# NOTES ON GENESIS II

*Lectures 26~49*

"When you do not have faith, everything becomes your responsibility.
However, if you have the faith to believe in God,
then all of these things are no longer yours but God's."

NOTES ON GENESIS Ⅱ

Bible quotations are from the King James Version of the Bible.

First Edition published in 2008

Published by Good News Publications, Inc.

606-45, Shinwol 2-Dong, Yangcheon-Gu, Seoul, Korea



For spiritual counseling, contact us at 1-888-GNN-9TIMES

ISBN 987-89-85422-97-0

ISBN 987-89-85422-95-6 (Set)

Printed in Korea

# Preface

Jesus went to Lazarus' tomb and said, "Thy brother will rise again. Take ye away the stone." But Martha replied, "Lord, by this time he stinketh: for he hath been dead four days." Jesus' words of, "Lazarus will awake for he is sleeping," are completely different from Martha's thought that he is already rotting and stinks and hence completely unable to rise again. Ultimately, Jesus' words were right because Lazarus did come back to life.

In the Bible, the thoughts of man differed completely from the thoughts of God whenever they met and conversed with one another. Lazarus is said to be dead because man sees through his own standard. On the contrary, when he is seen through Jesus' standards, he was not dead but merely asleep. Through the book of Genesis, God wants to crumble our standards and instill within us His standards. The earth was without form, void, and in deep darkness, but the earth became bright, bloomed with flowers, was filled with birds flying, and became a paradise when the Word of God came upon it.

Even now God wants to create a beautiful world where flowers bloom and fruits are borne in our heart, which is like the earth that was without form, void, and in darkness. Nevertheless, many people do not accept this will of God. They only insist, "I have too many sins! I am absolutely hopeless! I have nothing but despair!" Still, there is hope, power, and light inside of Jesus. Furthermore, there is life and there is love.

Now, as we read Genesis together, verse by verse, through this book, we will discover the heart of Jesus within the words. Although it is a love that cannot be understood with man's thoughts, if we accept this love that is inside of Jesus, and although it is a power we cannot understand, if we accept this power by faith, God will work exceedingly. We are dirty, filthy, and evil but Jesus is holy, true, and righteous. We need to accept the righteousness of Jesus because we do not have righteousness. However, many people do not realize this and try to become righteous with their own efforts. For such people, Genesis expounds the principles of spiritual life in great detail.

I am so thankful and overwhelmed that the "Notes on Genesis," which ran in *The New York Times* for two years have been brought together to be published as a book. I would like to thank the people of *The New York Times* who helped these messages run biweekly for two years.

I cannot forget the first Bible Crusade we had at Madison Square Garden in 2006 through the fervent request of the readers of the "Notes on Genesis." Through its success we have been continuing to have Bible crusades at Madison Square Garden every year, and I saw many people listening to the word, gaining the assurance of being born again, and rejoicing. All of this has happened through the will of God who loves the English speaking souls, and we believe that God will work beautifully through this book as well.

If the readers of this book, one by one, throw their standards away and accept the Word of God and enter into the word, the world of God will be formed in their hearts to lead them to the beautiful life of blooming flowers and bearing fruit.

July 12th, 2008
Pastor, Good News Gangnam Church

Ock Soo Park

# CONTENTS

# 26

## *How Did They Become Men of Faith?*

*And God said unto Abraham, As for Sarai thy wife, thou shalt not call her name Sarai, but Sarah shall her name be. And I will bless her, and give thee a son also of her: yea, I will bless her, and she shall be a mother of nations; kings of people shall be of her. Then Abraham fell upon his face, and laughed, and said in his heart, Shall a child be born unto him that is an hundred years old? and shall Sarah, that is ninety years old, bear? And Abraham said unto God, O that Ishmael might live before thee! And God said, Sarah thy wife shall bear thee a son indeed; and thou shalt call his name Isaac: and I will establish my covenant with him for an everlasting covenant, and with his seed after him.*
(Genesis 17:15~19)

## If So, I Too . . .

Many people say that spiritual life is very difficult. There are many people who handle computers well or play the piano with expertise, but I have never met anyone among Christians who say they are confident in their spiritual lives. Why is that so?

As I read the Bible, I thought about how the men of God, such as Abraham, David, Paul, and Peter became men of faith. When we look carefully into their lives, we see that they were not people of faith to begin with. Abraham, also, was a tremendously faithless man, as were Noah, Moses, and David. That was how they all were. The Bible records in detail how they lived ordinary lives but one day became people of faith.

When I read the Bible, the stories of Noah becoming drunk

and naked, Abraham lying and saying that his wife was his sister, Abraham taking a handmaid and having a son with her, David taking Uriah's wife and sleeping with her, and many other such stories were very encouraging. I always thought that I did not live my spiritual life well because I was lacking and weak. But as I saw the flaws of Abraham, Noah, and David, I came to know that they were no different from me, and I felt that I, too, then can live a life of faith.

In the book of Mark, the disciples hear from some women that met Jesus after He resurrected. However, no one believed those words. I was curious as to why this was because Jesus had often said while He was alive that He would be crucified and resurrect after three days. So then, when they saw Jesus being crucified, the disciples should have thought, "Jesus said that He was going to die, and so He is. He also said that He will resurrect in three days, so He will." Yet, none of the disciples believed the words of those who saw the resurrection. Thomas later says, "Except I shall see in His hands the print of the nails, and put my finger into the print of the nails, and thrust my hand into His side, I will not believe." I feel that even we would not have felt that way, and that the disciples were truly despairing people. But it is so amazing how they could change into such powerful servants and men of faith.

I always lived blaming myself. "What is wrong with me? Why am I so weak-willed? Why do I not have any faith and am so bad at living spiritual life? Why do I keep falling into sin and making mistakes?" As I saw myself, I often thought, "I cannot live a spiritual life." However, as I read the Bible, I discovered that the men of God were not perfect or brilliant people but were all the same filthy, sinful, lacking, weak, and pitiful human beings like I was. As I discovered that, I was not so different from Abraham or Jesus' disciples. I thought, "Then all a person like me has to do is properly learn spiritual life!"

## Man, Whose True Image Is Dirty

When we look at the steps taken by the people of faith in the Bible, their blemishes are not hidden but are recorded in detail just as they are. Seeing those things, I gained hope in my heart, and I became curious to learn how they, who were so evil and pitiful, became people of faith. Then I looked through the Bible and, person by person, the process was precisely shown.

When I read about the life of David, I envied him because he was bold, manly, and a man of faith while I am narrow-minded and vulgar. But one day, I saw David who committed adultery with Uriah's wife. And when he saw that she was pregnant, he wanted to hide it. Then he called her husband from the battle and said, "Go and sleep at your home tonight." He was doing this so that when the child would be born later, it would seem as if that was how the child was conceived. However, when Uriah did not go home, David made Uriah drunk to get him to go home, but that did not work either. Then David had Uriah killed on the battlefield. We can see that this David is not the bold, broad-hearted David, but a narrow-minded, low, and ruthless human being.

"Ah, that was the kind of man David originally was. He was bold and broad-hearted through receiving the heart of God. His real image is that he was a low, vulgar, narrow-minded, and dirty human being!"

I could clearly see David's true image.

## A Turning Point

Then how was David able to obtain faith? How was Noah, Abraham, Paul, or Peter able to obtain such faith? They all have something in common in their lives, and it was the fact that they all had a turning point. The Scriptures I am talking about today are talking precisely about that.

Abraham followed the Word of God, left his kindred, his country, his father's home, and went to the land of Canaan that God directed him to. But when a famine hit the land, he followed his own thoughts rather than the Word of God and went to Egypt. On his way there, he saw how beautiful his wife was. He felt that the Egyptians would kill him in order to take his wife. So rather than seeking guidance from God, he used a humanistic method, telling his wife, Sarah, "Say that you are my sister." In addition, when he did not have a child after 10 years had passed since he received the promise of God that he would have a son, he thought, "I guess God is not giving me a son. I would then rather listen to my wife and take her handmaid in order to have a son." He lived relying on his own thoughts rather than relying on the guidance or the promise of God.

But God appeared unto Abraham when he was 99 years old.

*Neither shall thy name any more be called Abram; but thy name shall be Abraham: for a father of many nations have I made thee.* (Genesis 17:5)

*And God said unto Abraham, As for Sarai thy wife, thou shalt not call her name Sarai, but Sarah shall her name be. And I will bless her, and give thee a son also of her: yea, I will bless her, and she shall be a mother of nations; kings of people shall be of her.* (Genesis 17:15-16)

What God was saying was so different from Abraham's thoughts. Abraham thinks that since he is almost 100 years old and Sarah is almost 90 years old and it has ceased to be with her after the manner of women, she cannot have a child. However, God says that she can have a child. Here, these two thoughts collide against one another. It was so definite to Abraham that he could not have a son, and therefore, he could not accept the Word of God. Think about it. Abraham was old, Sarah was old and it had ceased to be with her after the manner of women. She had no strength to conceive a child. However, God spoke: "Not so. Your wife, Sarah, shall surely have a son, and you shall call his name Isaac."

Now Abraham was confronted with the problem of deciding whether to accept the Word of God or proceed with his own thoughts.

We, too, need to think about this. I lived believing in myself before I started living a life of faith. I thought that if I tried, I could do it. I thought if I tried to keep the law, I could, and that I could live spiritual life as well if I tried. But as a result of my zealous efforts, I came to realize that it cannot be done through my determination, and that there were wrong aspects about my decisions. As I came to discover that I could not be trusted, little by little, I began to feel regretful towards myself. Before this happened, I had completely believed in myself and simply went forward according to what I thought. But as I came to have a heart of regret and despair, I was able to accept the Lord into my heart.

There are no problems when the heart of God and my heart are the same. It is a problem when they are different. In such times, I used to live following after my thoughts. But one day, I came to know that I was a pitiful, low, and evil human being. I was then able to distrust myself when the Word of God collided against my thoughts, and the Word of God was able to enter me.

## Something That Happens Where There Is the Work of God

God said, "Your wife, Sarah, will surely have a son, and you shall call his name Isaac," and Abraham thought, "It is impossible to have a child because I am too old and my wife is too old." Here, these two thoughts strongly collide against one another. At this moment, a person who believes in himself will exert his own thoughts until the end, and he will follow his own thoughts rather than follow the Word of God. But the people who saw how they have made mistakes and how they have sinned lose strength in their heart and receive the Word of God.

When Abraham was able to accept the Word of God, and when his heart to believe in himself was changed, then his thoughts and his judgment crumbled down as he heard the Word of God. He had moved from his thoughts to the thoughts of God.

Noah had first put all expectations for his life on earth.

However, one day God appeared to Noah and said, "I will judge the world with water, so go and make an ark." Upon hearing these words, Noah's heart moved. Everything on earth was already dead, and only the things that were inside the ark lived. Noah not only moved his heart into the ark, but moved everything that was his into the ark as well, and he did not leave a single thing on this earth. Likewise, we need to move our thoughts from the world of our heart to the world of the Word of God.

For people who so surely believe in themselves, this is impossible, but when you experience and measure yourself, you see that you are someone not worthy of being believed. When you realize that your heart is filthy, dirty, and deceitful, then you can deny yourself and accept the Word of God. Afterwards, regardless of how correct your thoughts appear to be, you will accept the Word of God to be correct.

This is so with all the stories of the Bible. When the wedding at Cana of Galilee ran out of wine in John chapter 2, Jesus told the servants of that house to fill the waterpots to the brim with water. When the waterpots were filled, He said, "Draw out now, and serve unto the governor of the feast." The servants could not understand this. "This is water. How can we serve this?" They cannot do this work when they have their own thoughts. But the servants denied their thoughts and accepted the words of Jesus. At that moment, the servants were able to experience the miracle of the water turning into wine.

There is something that happens in all places where the works of God appear. It is your thoughts being denied and you accepting the Word of God.

## The Two Attitudes in Receiving the Word

Although they open and read the Bible, people who believe in their own thoughts understand the Bible through their own thoughts, and thus, the meanings they gain are completely different from the Bible. On the other hand, people who have emptied themselves accept the word as it is, and the words become graceful.

Who does not know the fact that Jesus was crucified to forgive our sins? Everyone knows this. But although people know, those who have their own thoughts say, "It is true Jesus died on the cross for my sins, but I am a sinner because I have sinned." They add their own thoughts and that is the conclusion they arrive at. Such people continue to suffer in sin, but the people who completely throw their thoughts away and simply accept the Word of God are entirely different.

"I remember the sins I committed, and I do feel guilty. Nevertheless, I am righteous because the Word of God says that my sins are washed away and that I have been made righteous."

A certain man told his two sons that he would buy both of them a car. The older son, upon hearing this, thought, "Why is my father saying that? I know he can't afford it. He is only saying that to make me feel good." If that is how he believes, then there is no car in his heart. The second son told his friends, "Hey, I am getting a car. Let's go on a trip together." In his heart, he has a car already. Although the father said the same thing, the younger son, who accepted the words of his father exactly as they were, is completely different from the older son, who added his own thoughts.

God recorded in the Bible that He sent His son, Jesus Christ, and He forgave all of our sins. And He has called us righteous, holy, and clean. He said He does not remember our sins any more. If we accept these words as they are, we do not have sins. We are righteous and holy. But if you add your own thoughts to them, you will only say, "That's what the Bible says, but how could I so arrogantly say that I am righteous and holy? I have many sins. I have to wash my sins away."

## Simply Accept by Faith

Noah, Abraham, David, and the other men of faith were humans exactly like us. They, too, wanted to eat when they were hungry; wanted to drink when they were thirsty; wanted to enjoy themselves; and were sexually tempted. However, how did they become such people of faith? One day, they broke free from the condition of believing in their own thoughts. When the Word of God was different from their thoughts, they did not simply ignore it and proceed, but they examined it.

"God, I am one hundred years old, and Sarah is ninety. How can we have a child? I would that Ishmael may live before you."

"No. Your wife shall surely bear you a son. You will call his name Isaac."

Right then, Abraham's heart changed.

"That's right! God promised me a son, what is there He cannot do? Then I will have a son!"

In his eyes, it was clear that he could not have a son. But when he erased his thoughts and accepted the heart of God, a strong conviction that he would have a son took place in Abraham's heart. That is faith. When he had that faith, Sarah gained the strength to conceive. God's heart and our heart need to be connected through a channel, and our hearts need to become one. If God says that you will have a son and you say that you cannot have one, then that is a heart that is different from God's. The heart of God cannot flow into yours, and you will collide with God. But if you break your heart and say, "Yes, I believe I will have a son," God's heart and your heart become one and the heart of God flows in you. Power flows together in that heart and the strength to conceive and have a son springs forth.

Loving folks, believing in God is throwing your thoughts away and believing. It is not merely accepting the parts that fit your thoughts. Although you appear dirty, evil, lustful, and deceitful, if God has called you righteous, you are righteous. Throw all your thoughts away and say, "God has called me righteous. Then all my sins are washed away, and I am righteous!" and simply accept that by faith. That is how all the men of faith became men of faith. I hope that you will throw your thoughts away and become people of faith who believe in God.

# 27

# *True Repentance; an Absolute Necessity in Spiritual Life*

*Then Abraham fell upon his face, and laughed, and said in his heart, Shall a child be born unto him that is an hundred years old? and shall Sarah, that is ninety years old, bear? And Abraham said unto God, O that Ishmael might live before thee! And God said, Sarah thy wife shall bear thee a son indeed; and thou shalt call his name Isaac: and I will establish my covenant with him for an everlasting covenant, and with his seed after him.* (Genesis 17:17-19)

## Upon Discovering that My Nature Is Dirty and Evil

I often saw God changing my heart in my spiritual life. In the past, I considered all of my thoughts to be correct and pursued whatever I judged and decided upon. However, there is one thing that has changed since I have come to know God: I deeply realized how wrong my thoughts, which I had once deemed to be correct, actually were when reflected upon the Word of God.

True spiritual life is only achieved through "repentance" and "faith." It is important to say, "I have committed theft. I have committed adultery. I have lied. I have hated others," and turn from such sins. However, even more important than this is to discover the fact that your heart, itself, is dirty and evil. And you must turn away from your own heart.

I could not open my heart to others because I always lived with dirty, filthy, and evil thoughts in my heart. Because I thought of myself as a great person, although I was deplorable, I constantly had to hide myself. In reality, I was a filthy, dirty, and evil person, but I thought I could do good if I tried. I labored and toiled to live honestly as a good person. However, I failed time and time again. I thought, "Why doesn't it work? This time I'll do well," and I put my heart into doing well. But I failed. Amidst all this, I discovered that my nature was dirty, filthy, and evil. Therefore, trying to do good was just an act to cover up my deplorable heart and appear to be good. I came to know that, in reality, I cannot help but sin. The various sins I have committed in my life were not the actual problems. I realized that I could not live according to the will of God with this wicked heart. In turn, the grace I received when I threw my thoughts away and received the heart of God was tremendous.

## My Heart and Jesus' Heart

I once was invited by the church of a leper colony to preach the Word of God there. I had never been to a village where only lepers lived. It was to be my first time staying in a leper colony and preaching the gospel for an entire week. But as the date of the conference neared, I began to become worried in my heart.

"How will I eat and sleep when I go there? Will they ask me to eat with them? Will they want me to sleep in a room with lepers?"

One day, I woke up early in the morning and as I prayed to the Lord, I thought about the problem of going to the leper colony. The Lord then gave me these words:

*Now when Jesus was in Bethany, in the house of Simon the leper. . . .* (Matthew 26:6)

These words came to my mind, and then I thought, "The

precious and holy Lord went to the house of a leper. Then why should a pitiful and lowly person like me hesitate to enter a leper colony?" My heart changed. Worrying and being afraid was my own heart. I could feel that this new heart was not my heart but the heart of Jesus.

In addition, I thought, "Lepers are not special people. You will have a cold if you catch a cold. You will have tuberculosis if you catch tuberculosis. Likewise, I will become a leper if I catch leprosy." Before this I had thought that I was clean and the people who lived there were dirty lepers. But that difference vanished and it felt as though I could hug and kiss the lepers without hesitation. I visited the leper colony with this heart and the conference turned out wonderful. The doors of the gospel were opened to ten leper colonies and I continued to hold many conferences. I saw many lepers receiving salvation and I received much grace in my heart.

My original heart was to be distant from the lepers, but the heart of Jesus was to be completely free with the lepers. I, too, was able to freely stay with the lepers when that heart of Jesus entered me.

Before this happened, I labored for a long time to be good with my original heart. For a short time, it seemed as if goodness was appearing. Then, my original dirty and lustful hearts would arise. Thus, my life was always striped and spotted with filth, and I lived my life as a churchgoer feeling guilt in my conscience. I would then continue to tearfully confess my sins to God. However, one day God showed me my heart:

*The heart is deceitful above all things and desperately wicked:* (Jeremiah 17:9)

That was how my heart was in the eyes of God, but it was

not so in my own eyes. I would acknowledge that my heart was a little filthy, dirty, and evil, but I could not acknowledge this to the extent of me being called deceitful above all things and desperately wicked by the Word of God. One day, when I took a good look at myself, I discovered that this was truly the kind of person I am. It was then that my heart and the way that God saw me became the same.

"I am indeed dirty, deceitful, evil, and lustful. And because this is my nature, with my heart, I can never live as a goodly person, nor can I please God!"

After having this heart, I was able to deny myself. As I completely denied the heart to believe in myself and all of my thoughts, I was able to simply believe in the Word of God. Then the Word began to enter me. From then on, I lived being led by the Word.

## Abraham, Who Trusted in Himself

I was able to discover the clear reasons behind how the people of God became powerful people when I read the Bible. Abraham, David, Elijah, Daniel, Paul, Peter. . . . They all went through the process of their hearts of believing in themselves crumbling down, and they then moved into the position of trusting God throughout their lives. We can see that God began to work in them from that point onward.

God sincerely wants to work upon each and every person, but most people dwell within the frame of their own thoughts. Therefore, they cannot accept things that are outside of their thoughts, although it may be the Word of God. Then one day, when they realize that they are dirty and evil and throw their thoughts away, they can enter the Word of God. God can appear and work through them because now their hearts are the same as God's.

The Scriptures we are talking about today have recorded in detail such a change in Abraham. Abraham left Ur of the Chaldees according to the Word of God. Abraham did leave his country, his kindred, his father's house, and had entered Canaan, but his thoughts always remained within the frame of his own mind.

God appeared to Abraham when he was 99 years old and said, "I am the almighty God. Do not call yourself Abram but Abraham. I will multiply you greatly, and I will bless you so that your wife Sarah may bear you a son."

What did Abraham do upon hearing this? He thought having a son would be impossible because he had yet to be freed from the frame of his mind. He was 99 years old, and his wife was 89 and it had ceased to be with Sarah after the manner of women. When thinking about this, not from God's perspective, but from his own frame of mind, this was something that made no sense at all:

*Then Abraham fell upon his face, and laughed, and said in his heart, Shall a child be born unto him that is an hundred years old? and shall Sarah, that is ninety years old, bear? And Abraham said unto God, O that Ishmael might live before thee!* (Genesis 17:17-18)

This was purely Abraham's thought.

Isaiah chapter 55, verse 8 tells us, *For my thoughts are not your thoughts, saith the Lord.* The thoughts you have now are different from the thoughts of God. If so, is it your thoughts that are wrong or God's thoughts? Your thoughts are wrong. Nevertheless, people do not think that their thoughts are wrong. It is because those thoughts have come from what they have perceived, known, and experienced.

In his own eyes, Abraham's answer was the only reasonable one. How could a person 100 years old have a child? Sarah was ninety. It scares us to think that a 90-year-old woman would have a son. In our congregation, from time to time, there are women who become pregnant late in their lives or give birth for the first time in their 40's. The sisters all worry about their child's birth. Giving birth is difficult even for young women in their 20's and 30's. Having a first child in their 40's is extremely difficult. In light of that, isn't it scary to think that a 90-year-old woman would have a son? How could she endure the difficult labor?

Abraham's answer was very fitting when looked upon through the standards and judgments of man. This is the exact problem. Even though the thoughts you have may be normal and within the boundaries of common logic, they cannot be the same as the Word of God. Thoughts different from the Word of God are wrong.

There are many such cases when God was meeting man. It was so when God met Moses.

"Moses, I will send you to Pharaoh to lead my people of Israel out."

"No, I cannot do that."

Moses thought of his circumstances.

"I cannot do that. I am not eloquent. Send the one whom You will send."

"I will accomplish this work. I will send you to do this."

"No. . . ."

No matter who it may be, Satan pulls the current of our thoughts in the direction of not being able to accept the Word of God since we have been under the dominion of Satan from the time of Adam and Eve. However, God can easily be free of the rules of man and work because God is omnipotent. God can change the laws of the seasons. He can change everything in our lives, and if He does something, then it is accomplished. But we are unable to accept the Word of God because we are not freed from the frame of our thoughts. There, the problems in our spiritual lives begin.

## True Repentance Must Absolutely Come About

If the story were to end here, for the duration of his life, Abraham would not have been freed from the frame of his thoughts and he would still be living within them. However, God loved Abraham and approached him again, saying, *Sarah thy wife shall bear thee a son indeed; and thou shalt call his name Isaac: and I will establish my covenant with him for an everlasting covenant, and with his seed after him.* (Genesis 17:19)

Right then and there, Abraham changed his heart: "This was what I thought, but I will have a son if God allows it!"

Abraham's heart changed. That is the "repentance" which becomes the basis of spiritual life. Confessing that you have stolen, committed adultery, lied, or committed murder and turning from those things can be called repentance, but the most important thing in repentance is to turn from the heart to believe in yourself to the heart to believe in God.

In reality, we are not worthy of being trusted, but people trust in themselves because they love themselves. If you could see into your neighbor's heart like you can your own, you would feel so disgusted that you would not want to see that person again. But since it is you, you believe in yourself again and again. You are very understanding with yourself even though you make mistakes, and you trim your outward appearance to be good even when you sin. That is why you can go on living believing in yourself. Since everyone lives this way, it is very difficult for people to see their true image. And because they cannot see their own true image, they feel that they are right and follow their own thoughts. That is why they are unable to have faith.

Repentance must occur if true faith is to be formed in you. Not merely confessing the sins you have committed, but finally realizing, "My nature is so filthy and dirty. How could good ever come from me?" Because people do not know this, they deceive themselves and think that they can do good if they make the effort. They deceive themselves into thinking that if they try to follow the truth with their dirty, filthy, and evil heart, they can follow the truth. Thus, they try repeatedly, but it never works. And every time they fail, they repent again. Then they try once again, and of course they fail. Then they try again and fail again. Even though they continue to try until the day they die, they fail. In order for true faith to come to us, there has to be repentance not just from the wrong you have done, but repentance from yourself, as a whole.

People who are conned often are always conned because they trust the conmen. Conmen speak to gain people's trust, and their words seem credible; however, one will not trust a conman if the person knows his identity. He will not be deceived. We are being deceived by a conman named, "Me." Although you are a liar, you believe in yourself. Although you are dirty, you think that you can be good. Although you are evil, you think that you can believe in God well. Spiritual life cannot be formed in such states.

When you one day discover yourself, no matter who you are, you can distrust and be freed from your filthy and evil self. When you have the faith to believe in yourself, you will believe in your thoughts more than the Word of God when they differ from each other. On the other hand, when you distrust yourself, you can believe in the Word of God.

## You Also Need Genesis Chapter 17

When Abraham threw his thoughts away and entered the faith to believe in the Word of God, he was circumcised and changed his name from Abram to Abraham. From then on, God began to work inside of Abraham. Sarah gained faith as well. When the words that she will have a son took root in her heart by faith, the power of God was delivered, and this old woman gained new strength to conceive and bear a child.

Our spiritual life is exactly the same. You cannot create the earth with man's wisdom. You cannot create a human being with man's wisdom. A woman can have a child, but she cannot create one. All of this was done through the wisdom of God. When the wisdom and heart of God, which are beyond man's wisdom, take place in you, you can have a new heart of God that you have never had before. And when you have the same heart as God, He accomplishes His will.

Even with receiving the forgiveness of sin, we cannot crawl out from the pile of sin through our own strength.

"We eat and live amidst sin. How can we be as white as snow? How can we be clean?"

With your own thoughts, you can never become freed. However, God can free us from sin. People are unable to have faith in the forgiveness of sin because they only think at their level.

"Jesus was crucified, but I sin every day. How can I be righteous? I cannot say that I am clean."

But everything changes when they become freed from their own thoughts and reach the level of God's thoughts. They then have the heart that God has cleansed them.

"No matter how filthy I am, who is greater: God, who washes sins, or I, who commit sin? No matter how many sins I have committed, I am clean because the power of God is greater than my sins. My sins were all washed away at the cross. I am sanctified."

This is the heart they are able to gain through faith.

Abraham believed his own thoughts and judged everything. However, there came a time when his heart had changed. This was in Genesis chapter 17. You also need such an incident.

"I was wrong! My judgment was wrong! I cannot trust in myself! I should believe in God!"

Right then, no matter what you think, you can believe in God. The heart of God and your heart must become one in order for you to receive the grace of the Holy Spirit working powerfully.

Abraham was a man just like us. And just as he received the

grace of God to become the father of faith, when you become freed from your thoughts and accept the Word of God, you, too, will become a person of faith. Then the power of God will overflow in your life.

# 28

## *Live Experiencing Miracles*

*And he said, I will certainly return unto thee according to the time of life; and, lo, Sarah thy wife shall have a son. And Sarah heard it in the tent door, which was behind him. Now Abraham and Sarah were old and well stricken in age; and it ceased to be with Sarah after the manner of women. Therefore Sarah laughed within herself, saying, After I am waxed old shall I have pleasure, my lord being old also? And the LORD said unto Abraham, Wherefore did Sarah laugh, saying, Shall I of a surety bear a child, which am old? Is any thing too hard for the LORD? At the time appointed I will return unto thee, according to the time of life, and Sarah shall have a son.* (Genesis 18:10-14)

## To Experience Miracles

I have often experienced God accomplishing miraculous things that were absolutely impossible through man. One of them was being healed from a stomach ulcer. I had been suffering terribly from a gastric ulcer, and one day, I prayed to God to heal my stomach. Then God reminded me of the words, *What things soever ye desire when ye pray, believe that ye receive them, and ye shall have them,* from Mark chapter 11, verse 24 in my heart. If I believed that my stomach was healed as I had prayed, then just as these words said, I am supposed to be able to eat kimchi, dwenjang (Korean bean paste), and rice, but this was extremely burdensome. Then I thought about this objectively.

"If God says to believe that my stomach is healed, I do not need to add any thoughts of my own to this. Even though the circumstances are what they are, I will be healed if I believe that I am healed!"

From that morning on, I began to eat rice. I ate kimchi, dwenjang. . . . At first, I would have diarrhea and it was difficult, but I experienced my stomach becoming completely healed within 24 hours. Afterwards, my faith to believe in the Word of God became deeper, and God could work more powerfully through me.

There are miracles that have been recorded in the Bible. For example, there are the stories of Jesus turning water into wine; of the man who had an infirmity for 38 years rising up, taking up his bed, and walking; of lepers being completely cured; of the blind opening their eyes; of Jairus' dead daughter coming back to life, and many more. We call all of these occurrences miracles. But how could such miracles happen? If we know this precisely, we can draw such miracles into our own lives. We can receive the blessing and grace of accomplishing impossible things through the power of God.

All the miracles that appear in the Bible were accomplished by following the same principle. Therefore, if you can draw out this principle exactly in your own lives, you can experience the miracles of God in any aspect of your life. Through learning this, I have experienced impossible things being accomplished through the power of God numerous times. Such works can arise in your life as well, but not knowing this one thing is what is keeping you from the works of God occurring in your life.

## Principles for Achieving Miracles

Let us talk about, for example, Jesus turning water into

wine. How was this accomplished? When the wine ran out at the wedding at Cana, Mary said to Jesus, "They have no more wine." Jesus then replied, "Woman, what have I to do with thee? Mine hour is not yet come." However, Mary said to the servants, "Whatsoever He saith unto you, do it." Then Jesus told the servants to fill six empty waterpots with water. When they had finished filling the waterpots with water, Jesus said, "Draw out now, and bear unto the governor of the feast."

"This is water. How can we serve this? This is nonsense!" The thoughts of the servants could not go beyond this frame of mind. However, Jesus was saying to go serve it because this was not water but wine. But when the servants heard and accepted the words of Jesus, they were able to go beyond their thoughts, draw the water, and serve it. With their own heart, they could never draw out and serve it, but the miracle of the water turning into wine arose when they accepted the words of Jesus to draw out and serve. All the miracles achieved by God happen following such principles.

Jesus, one day, went to the pool of Bethesda. There was a man there who had an infirmity for 38 years. Jesus asked this ill man, "Wilt thou be made whole?"

"Sir, I have no man, when the water is troubled, to put me into the pool: but while I am coming, another steppeth down before me."

In these words he is probably meaning to say, "I don't know who you are but could you push me into the pool when the water is troubled?"

Jesus spoke to the ill man, "Rise, take up thy bed and walk."

This man had been lying down for 38 years with this disease. He cannot move even though he wants to enter the pool when the water is troubled. However, Jesus was telling him to take up his bed and walk. What thoughts do you think this ill man had?

"Are you telling me to walk? How can I walk? My legs are like logs of wood."

This was the original heart of this paralytic, but Jesus was saying that he could rise and walk. The hearts of the paralytic and Jesus were different.

"Are you telling me to take up my bed and walk? That is nonsense. I am a man who has had an infirmity for 38 years. I cannot move."

This was what he was supposed to say, but this did not happen. This was impossible in his thoughts, but he accepted the thoughts of Jesus.

The people of God know that their thoughts are crooked, filthy, and dirty. They therefore throw their thoughts away, accept the heart of Jesus, and live through that heart. The man with the infirmity for 38 years could never walk in his own thoughts. To walk was complete nonsense. It seemed that the words of Jesus were mocking him. However, he threw his thoughts away and decided to accept the words of Jesus. He believed that he could walk and began to rise. He began to roll his body over, and it began to move. He then pushed on the ground with his elbows and started to lift himself up. He was rising. Eventually, he stretched his legs and tried to stand. He stood. This was something that could never have been imagined within the thoughts of the man with the infirmity for 38 years. However, this was completely possible through the heart of Jesus entering his heart.

## If God Does It, Will It Not Be Done?

Because we are unable but God is able, the heart of the unable (us) and the heart of the able (God) cannot be the same. The thoughts of a person with a monthly salary of $10,000 cannot be the same as the thoughts of a person with a $1,000 monthly salary. If a person with a $1,000 salary spends money like the person with a $10,000 salary, he will immediately become bankrupt. Therefore, he must live according to his income. Likewise, your heart has solidified in living within your limits, and you cannot believe in the Word that goes beyond your limits. However, the moment you believe in God, the power of God goes beyond your limits to reach you because God is with you. Therefore, people who believe in God must think within the power of God.

Sadly, people are unable to do this. There is such a story in Genesis chapter 18. God spoke to Abraham, "Where is your wife, Sarah?"

"She is in the tent," replied Abraham.

"I will certainly return unto thee according to the time of life; and lo, Sarah thy wife shall have a son."

Sarah heard this at the door of the tent, and thought, "I'm going to have a son?"

Sarah had never once thought this. Sarah had already given up on having a child and gave her handmaid, Hagar, as a concubine to Abraham 14 years earlier. If she believed that she could have a child, what woman would allow another woman to enter her husband's bedroom? If there was a 0.1% chance for her to have a child, she would have put her hopes there. She would not have allowed another woman to enter her husband's bedroom. Sarah was certain that there was no means for her to have a child, and therefore, felt that she had no choice but to send another woman into her husband's bedroom.

That happened 14 years earlier, but now, 14 years later, God is saying to Abraham that Sarah will have a son. How can Sarah do anything but laugh? She laughed and said to herself, "After I am waxed old shall I have pleasure, my lord being old also?"

Right then God spoke to Abraham, "Wherefore did Sarah laugh, saying, Shall I of a surety bear a child, which am old? Is anything too hard for the Lord? At the appointed time I will return unto thee, according to the time of life, and Sarah shall have a son."

God scolded Abraham in front of Sarah.

Not long after the government was established in Korea, the President visited a base and had a conversation with a captain. The President saw greatness in this captain's thinking and said, "You, the rank you have on, what is it?"

"Sir, captain, sir."

"What is above that?"

"Sir, major, sir."

"What is above that?"

"Sir, lieutenant colonel, sir."

"What is above that?"

"Sir, colonel, sir."

"Be that."

From that day on, by the special command of the President, he became a colonel. Even the president of a country can do that. Isn't God the king of the universe? When God said,

"Have a son," then it is done. Whether it had ceased to be with Sarah after the manner of women, or whether she had surgery on her womb, or whatever, none of these things are problems whatsoever. She will have a son if God says that she will. We believe in the God who accomplishes impossible things. God wants to accomplish such miracles not only in the Bible but also in our lives.

However, in order for us to taste such works, we need to become freed from the limits of our thoughts. God worked upon Abraham, Sarah, and Moses to have man become freed from the frame of their thoughts. God wants to work in each one of us individually as well. God is not pleased with you doing some kind of good through your own power and labor, but He is pleased of your doing good and accomplishing the will of God through the power of God, which comes from receiving His heart. He does not want the things that come from our heart, which are by nature, dirty and filthy.

God made the prisoner Joseph into a governor, and He made David, the shepherd, into a king. If this God gives you wisdom, would you not become wise? He can even make you wiser than Daniel. If God makes you wealthy, will you not become wealthy? If God makes you healthy, will you not become healthy, no matter what disease you have? If God cleanses your sins, will you not become clean? The heart of thinking that it cannot be done even if God does it is a truly evil, cursed heart.

"Yes, it is impossible through humanistic means, but it can be done if you do it, God."

This is the heart of someone who believes.

"God, I am a dirty person who sins every day, but if you

make me clean I will be as white as snow. If you make me righteous and holy, I will be righteous and holy."

Isn't this the faith to believe in God?

Sarah laughed upon hearing that she will have a son. God then spoke to Abraham, "Wherefore did Sarah laugh, saying, Shall I of a surety bear a child, which am old? Is anything too hard for the Lord?"

Is there anything too hard for the Lord? There is nothing. If God does it, anything can be done. Sarah heard what God said and told Him, "I did not laugh." God said, "No, thou didst laugh," not acknowledging the words of Sarah, but establishing His Word. God does not acknowledge your words. God wants to establish His words in our hearts.

The heart to believe not in herself, but the faith to believe in God became established in Sarah's heart. God established this in her. When Sarah believed in God, she received the strength to conceive. A ninety-year old lady was springing up with strength, telling her servants, "Hey guys, let me carry that for you." This is a miracle. By faith, a miracle was upon Sarah. Sarah must have had many regrets later on. "How foolish I was! I thoughtlessly sent my handmaid into my husband's bedroom. I could have had the son myself."

## Receive the Heart of God

In the thoughts of the man with the infirmity for 38 years, he could not walk, but Jesus thought that he could take up his bed and walk. Sarah thought, "I can never have a son," while God thought, "No, you will have a son." Now, will you follow your own thoughts or the thoughts of Jesus? This is what's important. As Sarah threw her thoughts away and received the Word of God, the heart and power of God strengthened Sarah so that she lacked nothing in having a child.

I, too, was like this. I always thought, "I am a sinner. I can only commit sin. I'll be a sinner until the day I die. I am a sinner, but it would be nice if God would give me mercy for me to go to heaven." But God said, "No, your sins were washed away. Jesus already redeemed you. You are righteous. You have no sins." That is what the Bible says. *For all have sinned, and come short of the glory of God; Being justified freely by his grace through the redemption that is in Christ Jesus:* (Romans 3:23-24)

We are humans who have sinned, but God has already given the verdict that we are righteous, and we are clean because Jesus redeemed us. I could not believe this. I, for a long time, did not accept these words and only exerted my own stubbornness.

"Is anything too hard for the Lord?" Abraham and Sarah broke their own thoughts before these words and accepted the Word of God. Likewise, I too accepted the word before His voice.

"I sin every day, but could God not wash away my sins? Can the crucifixion of Jesus not wash away the sins of one person? Whether I sin one hundred times, or one thousand times, the sins I commit, Jesus must have washed them away. That's right! My sins are washed away!"

I was amazed. I am a person who cannot believe in such things, but a great miracle arose in my heart. I always sinned and thought that I was a sinner. I always thought that I had to suffer because of my sins and had to have my sins washed away.

But the miraculous thing was that I accepted the Word of God, which was different from the thoughts I had until then.

I accepted the heart of God. I believed it. This was not my heart, but the heart of God. After accepting these words, my heart became one with the heart of God, which said that my sins are washed away and I am righteous. From then on God began to work inside of me. Our hearts were different before because God said my sins were washed away, but I said that I had sins. However, as we became one, the Holy Spirit worked inside of me.

We learn from the Bible the process by which Abraham and Sarah were able to have the same heart as God. Now, you too should not believe in your thoughts, but in the Word of God. I hope you will accept the heart of God, no matter how much you have sinned, I hope that you will become free from sin through the faith to believe in Jesus who has cleansed you.

# 29

## *How Can You Become Righteous?*

*And he said, Behold now, I have taken upon me to speak unto the Lord: Peradventure there shall be twenty found there. And he said, I will not destroy it for twenty's sake. And he said, Oh let not the Lord be angry, and I will speak yet but this once: Peradventure ten shall be found there. And he said, I will not destroy it for ten's sake. And the LORD went his way, as soon as he had left communing with Abraham: and Abraham returned unto his place.*
(Genesis 18:31-33)

## Spiritual Life Is Difficult Without Clarity

Spiritual life, once you know what it is, is truly easy. Once we learn something at school and come to know something, it is easy, but when you don't, it is very difficult. Spiritual life, for the most part, is difficult because of the lack of clarity. People are deceived by Satan and simply think, "All I have to do is not sin according to the Word of God and be good, don't I?" If you could become good and have the ability to live according to the word, the Bible would only have to be a few pages long. It would only have to say, "Be good. Live according to the word. Then you'll be fine."

The Bible teaches us our image through completely revealing to us the world of our hearts. The conclusions we arrive at are different from the ones God arrives at. When I meet with people and speak to them about spiritual life, many say to me, "Pastor, although I am weak now, I think I can do well if I try. Right now, my heart is not settled and it is difficult but, when things do settle down, I will live as a good person." They think that it is that simple. The important thing is that it may appear on the surface to be this way, but they must know that we can never completely keep the Word of God.

## What Will You Do if There Are Ten Righteous?

God is talking to Abraham about the destruction of the cities of Sodom and Gomorrah in today's Scriptures. Here, it speaks of the "righteous." Abraham contended with God, saying, "God, will you destroy the city even if it has 50 righteous people? Should you not be fair when you are judging the world?" Just as it is written in 2 Peter, ". . . and delivered just Lot," Abraham's nephew, Lot, was a redeemed, righteous child of God. Abraham had assumed that since Lot, his wife, and his two daughters were living in the city, there were four righteous persons, so there must be at least fifty people who had received salvation through the four of them evangelizing.

Then God spoke.

"I will not destroy the city if there are fifty righteous there."

Upon hearing this, Abraham thought, "Why is God so willing to adhere to my proposal? I don't think there are fifty there. Then let me take away five."

Then he once again spoke to God, "Will you destroy the city if there are five people short?"

"No, if there are forty-five righteous, I will not destroy the city."

Abraham thought, "Does this mean that there are not even forty-five righteous people there?"

"What will you do if there are forty?" asked Abraham.

"I will not destroy the city," said God.
"What will you do if there are thirty righteous people?"
"I will not destroy the city."
"What will you do if there are twenty righteous people?"
"I will not destroy the city."

Finally, Abraham who had thought that there were at least 50 righteous people, spoke once again to God in a discouraged voice. "God, I will speak only this time. What will you do if there are ten righteous?"

"I will not destroy it for the sake of the ten," replied God.

Lot, who was saved, his wife, and his two daughters entered the city of Sodom. But rather than testifying of the grace of God to have ten people, twenty people, or fifty become righteous, the four of them fell into the world. This was the reason for God passing down destruction.

God is ready to destroy this world, but He is not doing so because He wants at least one more person to be saved and not destroyed. Nevertheless, the works of people being saved did not happen as Lot entered the city of Sodom. Rather, it was Lot who started falling more and more into the world. God did not feel the need to wait any longer. He decided to destroy Sodom. There were nowhere near fifty righteous people, needless to say ten, and lastly, when the judgment came upon Sodom and Gomorrah, Lot's wife was also thrown away and only three were delivered.

## Quickly Throw Away Trying to Be Good

Was Lot saved because he lived as a good person while he was in the city of Sodom? That was not so. Did he keep the law well? He did not do that at all. He became righteous through the grace of God. People do not know about this aspect very well so they only think, "If I listen to the word to be a good person and keep the law without sinning, I shall become righteous." This is a thought from a human perspective, but the image of man from God's perspective is, *the heart is deceitful above all things and desperately wicked.* (Jeremiah 17:9) In the eyes of God, there is no one who appears to be holy, righteous, or good.

*The Lord LORD looked down from heaven upon the children of men, to see if there were any that did understand, and seek God. They are gone aside, they are all become filthy: there is none that doeth good, no, not one.* (Psalms 14:2-3)

Man thinks that he can be good if he tries, but God says, "No, you humans have no good in you because you are filthy, dirty, and evil by nature." This is the difference between the thoughts of God and the thoughts of man.

Now man must submit to how God sees him. "Yes, if you say that there is none that is good, then that is right."

However, people try to be good because they feel that they can accomplish it if they try. God, on the other hand, says that there is no good in man, and that He could not find any goodness, righteousness, or holiness in any man. But seeing things from man's perspective, man disagrees with this.

"I am good. I did make mistakes, but still I am godly and holy."

This is the heart of man. Therefore God tells us to, "Quickly throw away your efforts to become good."

## If Korea Is on the Other Side, Let Us Dig Until We Get There

There was a missionary who once ministered to a South American Indio tribe called Nambikwara. This missionary had a chance to visit Korea and told the Indios, "I'll be visiting Korea for awhile." How could the Indios, who live in the jungle, know where Korea is?

"How far is Korea?"

"It is very far. On the globe, we are here, and Korea is completely on the other side. That is why I am taking an airplane there."

When the missionary explained this, one Indio said, "If we are here, and Korea is on the other side, why do you have to take a plane to get there? Just dig into the ground until you get there. As you dig, if there is water then you can drink it. And if you keep digging and reach Korea, you'll be there." That was what the Indios thought.

The Indios also have a very simple way of counting. One "cana cana." Two "ha-ri." Three is expressed as "ha-ri cana cana," and four is "ha-ri ha-ri." After that, there is no more. The rest is simply expressed as "many." They have no five, six, or even seven. If we tell these Indios that Korea is 11,000 miles from Brazil, how could they know a number as big as 11,000? They only express it as "many," or "far away." Since they have no idea how big the earth is, they simply think with the knowledge they have, which is that you can dig until you reach Korea.

We are more advanced in our numeric concept than the

Indios, but there is not much of a difference between us and them in the eyes of God. Although you may appear to be a little better than your neighbor; though you may be more honest than some church goers; everyone is the same in the eyes of God. We have all fallen into evilness and into sin. We just make up some goodness from within our filthy, dirty, and sinful nature and try to show that off. In spite of that, it disappears quickly. Because evil and dirty hearts continually spring up inside of man, God can never discover any goodness that comes from man.

There are many people who think that they are good, righteous, godly, and honest. It seems that way at man's level. We are able to do more good than our neighbors. We can be godlier than other people. We can even be more honest than someone who is always deceiving people. We can also be more truthful than a person who lies continually. All of these things are relative from man to man. You appear to be good when you judge yourself in this way, relative to others. Nevertheless, you are not good in the eyes of God.

## You Said that There Is None Righteous, and Now You Say There Is?

Romans chapter 3, verse 10 says, *There is none righteous, no, not one.* But the interesting thing is that the "righteous" are often mentioned in the Bible. *Noah was a just man.* (Genesis 6:9) It says that Noah was righteous. The Bible also says that Abraham was righteous. Lot was also recorded as a righteous person as in the words, *delivered just Lot,* in 2 Peter chapter 2, verse 7. The Apostle Paul also said, "I have righteousness." The

Bible also says, in James chapter 5, verse 16 that, *the fervent prayer of a righteous man availeth much.* The Bible also mentions "righteous Job."

As we can see, in the Bible, there are many righteous people. It is here where people feel confused. "The Bible says that there is none righteous, but why are there righteous people in the Bible?" People are unable to find an answer to this and simply conclude, "There is none righteous. I am a sinner until the day I die. The Bible says there is no one who is righteous."

However, when we look deeper into this, there is a precise answer. There is no one righteous among man because we humans are all filthy and dirty. If so, how did Noah become righteous? God is righteous. Therefore, the people who receive the righteousness of God are those who become righteous people. This is not their righteousness, but the righteousness of God. Apostle Paul said this in Philippians: . . . *not having mine own righteousness, which is of the law, but that which is through the faith of Christ, the righteousness which is of God by faith.* (Philippians 3:9)

## Because We Are Crooked and Evil by Nature

I had no idea that I had a crooked walk. I once went jogging, and for some reason, there was a large mirror there. I ran in front of the mirror and I could see that my left foot went forward properly, but my right foot swung outwards. Right then, I came to know that the way I walk was crooked. Afterwards, I tried to walk straight whenever this came to mind, but when I asked a doctor about this, he said, "Pastor, your leg muscles have already developed accordingly, so unless you constantly concentrate on this, you will subconsciously walk crookedly."

I can walk straight when I think to, but when I don't think about it, my right foot goes forward crookedly because my muscles have developed in a crooked way. This is how people are. Because people have crooked personalities, they have some images of goodness when they remember to be good, but quickly, they become crooked again. Because you are filthy, honest images come from you occasionally when you are trying to be truthful, but after a couple of steps, the filthy things come out from you. Dirty things, lustful things, and deceitful things come out from you as well. This person is not a proper person but a crooked person.

Man cannot become good when he is consciously trying to become good. While he may be honest and truthful, then, when he is not totally concentrating, he quickly becomes evil, dirty, and filthy. That person is evil. He is a crooked person. However, people remember for a long time the one good deed they have done, and think that they can live properly. They walk crookedly all of the time, but when they take one good step, they think, "I can walk straight." That is total nonsense.

A long time ago, a teacher was teaching English to children at a small school in a village. He could not pronounce, "Windy wind." Therefore, he said to them, "Repeat after me. Vindy vind." Then all the children said, "Vindy, vind." He said, "Hey kids, it's not vindy vind. It's vindy vind." Then the children again said, "Vindy vind." The teacher realized that his pronunciation was wrong. Then he said to the children, "Hey kids, even though I say, 'Vindy vind,' you guys should say, 'Vindy vind.'" This teacher could not say, "Windy wind," no matter how hard he tried.

## We Are Righteous Through the Righteousness of Jesus

That is exactly how we are. We cannot become righteous through our actions. We cannot do it no matter how hard we try. That is why we need to give up on ourselves and receive the righteousness of God. That is how Apostle Paul became righteous. Jesus committed righteousness and did not sin once during his 33 years of life on this earth. Jesus lived a holy life. On the contrary, we both ate and drank sin our entire lives. We could only be destroyed because of this. Hence, God gave us the holy righteousness of Jesus who had not sinned for all of His 33 years, while casting the dirty sins we committed throughout our lives upon Jesus. He made an exchange. We could never have been saved unless this was done. God cast all the sins we committed onto Jesus and gave to us the holy righteousness Jesus lived with.

Whether you wanted it or not or whether you know it or not, God has already accomplished this. Because our sins have moved over onto Jesus, Jesus became a sinner although He had not sinned. On the other hand, we became righteous through the righteousness of Jesus although we did not live righteously. It was not by my righteousness, but the righteousness of Jesus! This was achieved in heaven, in the heart of God, and in the heart of Jesus. Finally, this needs to become achieved in our hearts.

How could this become achieved in our hearts? Saying, "Ah, my sins have moved onto Jesus and were ended on the cross! I have the righteousness of Jesus, so I am righteous! That is why God called me righteous!" and realizing and accepting it into your heart is what achieves righteousness in your heart.

Nevertheless, people do not know this, and labor to become righteous through trying to live righteously.

It is impossible for us to become righteous through our efforts to be good. On the contrary, it is so easy to accept the righteousness that Jesus has achieved. There is no one who can become righteous through not sinning and committing righteousness, but it is very easy to become righteous if you accept what Jesus has done.

Can a woman make a child just because she wants to? She may draw out the image of a person in the dirt but how can she make blood vessels, a heart, and pour life into the drawing? A woman can have a child through receiving life from a man. Even if the woman cannot draw or sculpt well, she can have a truly beautiful child who has eyes, a nose, a heart, and everything else if she receives the seed from a man.

We cannot make righteousness with our efforts. However, we can have righteousness if we accept it. This is what God did for us. We do not become righteous through our efforts or good deeds, but He has us accept the righteousness of Jesus which was accomplished through a 33-year-long life without a single sin, and a life of righteousness. If we accept the life of Jesus, we are more righteous than anyone because we then have the righteousness of Jesus.

He did this whether you are good or bad, have zeal or no zeal, regardless. God did not care whether you were dirty, filthy, evil, or full of lies, but He gave you the righteousness of Jesus. He had Jesus take away all of your sins. He exchanged Jesus for your sins. Jesus, who was without sin, bore your sins and became a sinner. You became righteous through being clothed with the righteousness of Jesus. Jesus is righteous and we are sinners. But through this exchange Jesus became a sinner and we became righteous. As a testament of this, Jesus was crucified on the cross to shed His blood for your sins. When you accept this by faith, the righteousness of Jesus comes upon your heart, and you become righteous. Then it is extremely easy to become righteous.

## You Are Righteous if You Have Righteousness

It is not that we have to make righteousness, but we become righteous through receiving the righteousness of Jesus. Because Abraham realized this, he thought that Lot preached the Word of God to the people of Sodom while Lot was there. Abraham thought there would be at least fifty righteous people there. On the contrary, Sodom and Gomorrah were destroyed because Sodom did not even have ten righteous people.

Someone who has received the righteousness of Jesus is righteous. Who is rich? If someone inherits a lot of wealth from his father, he is rich. Even though you have no money, if you win the lottery and receive 10 million U.S. dollars, you are rich. Whether you made the money or not, you are rich if you have much money. In becoming righteous as well, whether it was you who made it or not, you are righteous if you have righteousness. We become righteous, not through our effort, but through receiving the righteousness of Jesus.

# 30

## *Lot Who Came to Save God*

*And they called unto Lot, and said unto him, Where are the men which came in to thee this night? bring them out unto us, that we may know them. And Lot went out at the door unto them, and shut the door after him, And said, I pray you, brethren, do not so wickedly. Behold now, I have two daughters which have not known man; let me, I pray you, bring them out unto you, and do ye to them as is good in your eyes: only unto these men do nothing; for therefore came they under the shadow of my roof.* (Genesis 19:5~8)

## Man Who Trusts in Himself

I have attended church ever since I was young. Back then, I did not know anything about the Bible, yet with the small Bible knowledge that I had, I just assumed that keeping the law and living honestly was doing well in spiritual life. But eventually, I felt the limits to that as I lived spiritual life. It did not work out no matter how hard I tried to do good, and I came to realize that my heart was dirty and evil. Afterwards, I received the grace of God and received salvation.

I became born again not because I did good deeds or was sincere, but actually because I was evil and wicked. "I cannot keep the law anymore. I cannot do anything good anymore. I cannot please God." This truth came strongly upon my heart one day. In other words, the heart to believe in myself came crumbling down, and amazingly, I was able to believe in God.

For a long time I had a strong heart to trust in myself and I decided everything by my own standards. Thus, when the words of God and my thoughts differed, my thoughts took priority over the words of God. There was no problem when the Word of God and my thoughts were the same, but when they differed, it seemed that I would fail if I followed the Word of God. It would have been nice to follow the Word of God, but it seemed that I would go through difficulties and be ruined so I followed my thoughts. Even so, I labored to be good. I thought, "I can go to heaven if I pray, read the Bible, and live as a good person. God will look favorably upon me." This was how I had thought.

In the Bible are many conversations between God and man. Abraham, Noah, Moses, and many others spoke with God. The unique element in all these conversations between God and man is that God always speaks as God and man always speaks from the human-centered perspective. Because man cannot see God and lives only in his own world, man appears to himself to be big. It appears to man that he has more power than he actually does, causing him to have unrealistic expectations on what he does.

## People Intoxicated with Themselves

There were not ten righteous people in the cities of Sodom and Gomorrah. Lot, rather than leading more people to receive salvation, was falling more and more into sin with his family. There was no need for Lot to remain at a place where people are not receiving salvation. Therefore, the angels went to that city to destroy it and save Lot. But when the angels arrived, the people of Sodom saw that some new people had come and went to Lot's house at night. They shouted for Lot, saying, "Lead those men out. We will know them." It means that they wanted to have sexual relations. Lot went out and closed the doors behind him and spoke to the men of Sodom. "My brothers, do not do this. These people have come to me, but I have two daughters that have not known men. I will give them to you and you do with them as you please. But do not do this to these men." Lot knew that they had come from God.

When I first read these words I thought that Lot was very good. I saw him going as far as to sacrifice his own daughters to protect the angels and I thought, "Wow, Lot has such a blessed heart. That was why he was saved." That was what I thought. However, as time passed and I reexamined those Scriptures, it was not so. Did Lot indeed save the angels? No, he did not. It is God who is supposed to save Lot. How could Lot save the angels of God?

People are self-indulgent and think of themselves as being great. They say, "I preached the gospel for God. I built a church for God," and they live being indulged by doing something for God. There are so many people like this. This is why they cannot receive what God has done for them. This is a big problem in their spiritual life. I, too, for a long time thought that I did many things for God. I read the Bible, woke up early to pray, taught Sunday school students. . . . Although I had many sins, I thought that if I did even more and better works, God would look upon these good deeds and receive me into heaven. However, later on, as I read the Bible, I came to know that God does not accept anything from man because we are dirty sinners. I also came to realize that anything I do for God is absolutely useless. I came to realize that I was such a shameful and foolish being before God.

You think that you do good and that you do many things

for God. Anyone who thinks that he can work for God is completely intoxicated with himself. Drunken people lose their sanity and cannot think logically and think of themselves as being great. People not only get drunk with alcohol, but they often become intoxicated with themselves. People who are intoxicated with themselves think that if they try to do something, they can do well; and if they do something, that thing will go well. They feel that if they get involved, then God's things will go well and the church will go well.

## Why Was Uzza Killed?

When David was bringing the ark into the city of David from the house of Abinadab in 2 Samuel, it was carried on a new cart. As they arrived at Nachon's threshing-floor, the oxen shook the cart and Uzza held on to it. God struck and killed Uzza on the spot. Many people ask me about this.

"The ark would have fallen over had Uzza not held onto it. Uzza held the ark to serve God. Why did God then strike Uzza?"

I always give the same answer. If there is one thing that could most dent God's pride, it would be that God survived through the help of man. If that were the case, then God would not be God. If the falling ark was preserved through Uzza's holding on to it, it means that man upheld God. Each time this happened, God coldly struck down the arrogant man.

"I did something for God; I did something for the church; I built this church; what would happen to the church if I'm not here?" All of these are cursed thoughts.

## God Is Not a Salesman

I once went to a hospital and a person there who was terminally ill said this to me: "Pastor, pray for me. If I am healed of this illness, I will give half of my wealth to God."

I replied to him, "Sir, if you do that, God will curse you."

"What? What do you mean?"

"Do you think God is a salesman receiving money if He heals you? This is what God hates the most. When God gives something to man, He does not do so through wages but He wants to bestow grace freely."

Man can only receive the grace of God. God gave us our bodies, the rain, air, sunlight. . . . We do not pay $50 for a pretty nose, $30 for a flat nose, $20 for a pig-shaped nose like we pay extra for an air conditioning option on a car, do we? We have received our bodies through grace. God sent His son, Jesus Christ, to this earth to be crucified in order to forgive our sins. This was given to us through grace. We did not pay any kind of wage whatsoever. God is not a salesman. "I did this, so help me. I gave a tithe, so bless me." This is what offends God the most. When a beggar is asking for alms, he must say, "If you do not bestow grace upon me, I can only starve. Have compassion on me and bestow grace upon me. Please give me some money." This is the attitude of a beggar. If a beggar says, "I will pay you $1,000 later, so give me food right now!" That person is not a beggar but an extortionist.

When we go before God, we are people who could only have been cursed and who do nothing well. Even if there is something you do well, it is nothing before God. There is nothing good you can present. That is why we must simply receive the grace God gives through His compassion for us. "God, my life ended here because I was sick, but I will be thankful if You will bestow Your grace upon me and heal my disease." Saying this is the correct attitude. "Heal me because I will pay this much money." This is paying a wage, not receiving grace. Grace can only be grace when it does not require any sort of wage.

I said to the ill man, "Sir, God is not pleased with that. Do you think God is in suffering because He has no money? I think it is good that you are offering a large sum of money, but God isn't happy about that. God hopes that you would say, 'I am a person who can only be destroyed. Have compassion on me and bestow Your grace upon me and save me.' God is pleased with that."

God hates it the most when we say, "Save me since I have done good." "Help me since I have been loyal to You." "Bestow Your grace on me because I have done this and that." Therefore, when we come to God, we must come empty-handed, seeking grace and mercy.

## There Is No Path to Salvation Other than Grace

When God was about to destroy the cities of Sodom and Gomorrah, He went there to save Lot and his family. Foolishly, Lot tried to save God himself. He tried to protect God. This is what God hates the most. He wants to teach us this.

When God saves man, He does so without receiving any help from man. It is this way in each salvation story. The prodigal son did not become clean through doing something himself when he returned to his father. He was wearing filthy rags and returned as a starving beggar. But the father cleaned him up, sanctified him, and made him whole. There is nothing the prodigal son added whatsoever. It was 100% of the father. The filthy rags were removed and new clothes were put on him, a ring was placed on his hand, new shoes were put on his feet, the fatted calf was killed and fed to him. All of this was through the father.

This is also true with the parable of the man who fell among thieves. There was a certain man who fell among thieves as he was on his way from Jerusalem to Jericho. A Samaritan happened to be passing that way, saw him, and had compassion on him. The Samaritan approached him, poured oil and wine over the wounds, bound him up, put him on his beast, took him to an inn, and took care of him. Then the next day, he gave two pence to the inn keeper and said, "Take care of him. If you spend more, I will repay you when I come again." There is nothing the man who fell among thieves did to receive salvation. All he did was realize that he was a man who could only die and left himself to the Samaritan.

What did the man who fell among thieves think? "The priest passed me by and so did the Levite. Unless he bestows his grace upon me and saves me, I can only die!" He only had hope in the Samaritan and looked to him.

Likewise, there has to be no way other than the blood of Jesus and the grace of the Lord for us to receive the grace and mercy of God. However, people are foolishly deceived by Satan and think that if they do good and work for God, God will save them. There are so many people who, in this way, put hope in themselves.

Lot's trying to save God was all vain labor. Lot offered his daughters to the men of Sodom, but they still tried to tear his door down. Lot failed in trying to save God and God began to work from that point on. He blinded all the men who were outside. Then He told Lot to escape quickly. As Lot lingered, God held his hand and led him to a safe place. Lot's attempt to save God failed, but the salvation accomplished by God was achieved. Everyone, we are truly dirty sinners who can only be destroyed. That is why we have to receive grace. The person who has the most faith is the person who seeks the grace of God and leaves himself to God to be led by Him.

## I Served for 14 Years in Prison, so Why Can't I Go to Heaven?

I once went to Vietnam and met a pastor from an underground church. He was a person who had been imprisoned for 14 years for Jesus. I wondered how, for 14 years, he could keep his faith and not betray God. He was very admirable. However, as I spoke with him, I was startled. He believed that he could go to heaven because he kept his faith in prison for 14 years. It is something tremendous to serve 14 years, but how could that compare to the cross of Jesus? However, in his heart, his service in prison for 14 years was greater than the blood Jesus shed.

"I suffered and was in anguish for the Lord here in prison. My family suffered so much. Of course I am saved."

He was zealously loyal, but he did not know the Bible. I explained it to him in detail.

"Salvation is not achieved through our works. We are not saved because we do something. It is through the grace of Jesus."

He did not want to accept this.

"You! Have you been imprisoned for 14 years? Try it! Do you know how hard it is? I kept my heart through this. Why can't I go to heaven?"

"No. We can never be saved by works no matter what our works are. If we could be saved through some work one hundred times, one thousand times greater, it would not have been necessary for Jesus to be crucified. However, because we cannot do it, Jesus was crucified. We are evil by nature and God has already scored us as 'evil.' Now we need to receive the righteousness of Jesus in order to be righteous. It cannot be through our own actions."

I saw how disappointed he became as he listened to what I said. The rich young man went away in anxiety upon hearing the words of Jesus, and this man, too, went away in anxiety because he felt he had done so much for God.

## Out from Lot's Foolishness and Hoping in God

You must have nothing when you come before God. In reality, we have nothing. However, Satan makes it seem that if we bring forth a few things we have done well and our goodness, God will accept them. Satan makes us believe in this to keep us from trusting in Jesus.

Everyone, we have been categorized as evil before God.

*There is none righteous, no not one . . .* (Romans 3:10)

God is the only one who is good. That is why we must become a part of Jesus. You are good when you have the things of Jesus. Our goodness seems good in our eyes, but it is nothing in God's eyes.

Lot foolishly tried to save God by himself, but God saved Lot instead. Now let us stop foolishly trying to do something for Jesus, like Lot, in order to be rewarded. I hope that we will realize that our actions are nothing before God but are empty and deny everything of ours. Jesus said, "Whosoever will follow me should deny himself." A person who denies himself must deny every action of his as well. This is denying yourself. You must deny yourself and accept into your heart what Jesus has done for you. Then when you put hope and faith in what Jesus has done and come before God, you can receive the grace of God and gain eternal life.

# 31

# *Pit Your Thoughts Against the Word of God*

*And the LORD visited Sarah as he had said, and the LORD did unto Sarah as he had spoken. For Sarah conceived, and bare Abraham a son in his old age, at the set time of which God had spoken to him. And Abraham called the name of his son that was born unto him, whom Sarah bare to him, Isaac. And Abraham circumcised his son Isaac being eight days old, as God had commanded him.* (Genesis 21:1-4)

## If You Know the Law of Faith . . .

Spiritual life is something that is truly easy, fun, and blessed. It is quite easy if you know the law of spiritual life, but there is nothing as unclear, difficult, and tiring as spiritual life when you do not know the law of spiritual life. In other words, spiritual life is believing in God because it cannot be accomplished through the power of man. When doing something through faith in God, one should not calculate whether it is possible, but should think, "Can God do this, or not?" We believe in God when we cannot do something with our humanistic efforts. However, within this belief, believing when things seem possible in your calculations while not believing when things seem impossible, is not believing in God.

Abraham had two sons. One was Ishmael, born of a handmaid, and the other was Isaac, born of faith in God. Abraham had no faith in God when he had Ishmael; he was old and so was his wife, and he judged that he could not have a child. However, that was his judgment. No matter how old he is, if God wants him to have a child, can he not have one? Abraham and Sarah thought in their humanistic judgment, "We cannot have a child. It saddens us to do this, but we shall have a child through the handmaid," because they had no faith in God. The distrust that God would not give them a son worked inside their heart.

Why does distrust form in your heart? It is because faith does not take place in your heart. "Is it I or God who will have me father a son?" It was not Abraham who was allowing a son to be born. "That's right! It is God who would allow a son to be born. There is nothing God cannot do. Why would He not allow me to father a son?" This faith is all he needed, but his heart shook because he did not have this faith although God promised him a son. It seemed that he could not have a son when he thought of the circumstances. Therefore, he took a young and healthy handmaid, someone who seemed that she could deliver a child well, to give birth to a son. This son was the son borne of distrust, Ishmael.

Much time had passed after the birth of Ishmael. In fact, it was 13 years afterwards that Abraham had Isaac. Abraham and Sarah were older, and it had ceased to be with Sarah after the manner of women. It seemed absolutely impossible that they would have a child. That is why Abraham and Sarah laughed when God said that they would have a son.

"Shall a child be born unto him that is an hundred years old? And shall Sarah, that is ninety years old, bear?"

But they did have a son. How was that so? "Surely this is impossible, but since there is nothing God cannot do, it can be done if He does it." They were able to have a son because this faith arose in their heart.

As I, too, live a life of faith, I often face circumstances like that of Abraham having a son. "This is absolute nonsense!

Impossible! There is no way this can be done!" This is the judgment I often arrive at. However, after a little while, when God gives me thoughts, I say, "This is impossible, but if God does it, it can be done!" and I add a little more to what I thought before. Spiritual life truly became easy after I learned this.

### My Heart and the Heart God Leads

When I entered the military and was training at the training center, I one day lost my gloves. In the army, this was a huge problem. There was no way for me to replace them. Right then, Satan continually spoke to my heart: "This is the army. Where can you get gloves? There is no way for you to get any. However, there is one way. When everyone is sleeping, steal the pair of the person next to you. Yours were stolen, so don't think of this as stealing. This is how army life is." These thoughts strongly entered my heart.

I often felt in my spiritual life that the flow of my thoughts differed from the direction in which God leads my heart. I was then able to think, "This is how my thoughts are, but I wonder what God's thoughts are," and received much grace although I was, from time to time, led by my thoughts. Even though I thought of stealing the gloves, I experienced a complete change of heart: "I am now starting my military life. Suppose I do steal a colleague's gloves and get caught. Then no matter how my army life goes over the next three years, my life of witnessing here is absolutely over!" When I arrived at this conclusion, I decided that I would rather suffer for having lost the gloves, and the heart to steal completely disappeared from me.

We have our own heart, and there's the heart led by God. Not being able to have a son was originally the heart of Abraham and Sarah. Therefore, they took her handmaid to have Ishmael. But after 14 years passed, it seemed even more impossible that they would have a son. However, God put a thought inside Abraham: "Is anything too hard for the Lord? Why did Sarah laugh? Your wife, Sarah, will surely have a son, and thou shalt call his name Isaac."

Right then the Word of God entered the heart of Abraham and Sarah, and the faith, "That's right! It is humanly impossible but if God gives us a child, why will we not have one?" arose in them. That faith gave Sarah the strength to conceive, and ultimately, they had Isaac according to the Word of God. This Isaac became the father of many nations like the stars in the sky and the sands of the seashore.

## This Is My Thought, but What Would God Say?

You always flow towards your thoughts as you live your spiritual life. It is only natural that you flow that way, but I am urging you to ask the question, "This is my thought, but what would God say?" after you arrive at your conclusions. Then, when you lay down your thoughts and the Word of God on the table and say, "Which one of these two is correct? Of course God is correct," and select the Word of God rather than your thoughts, the works of God begin.

Humanistic thoughts arise in you to lead your heart to a side opposite of the Word of God, and this is true with everyone. The important thing at this point is to hold your thoughts for a moment and then think, "This is what I think, but what does the Word of God say?"

This is something I often talk about. The wedding at Cana of Galilee was short of wine. Right then, Jesus told the servants there to fill some waterpots with water. When they did so, He said, "Draw out now and serve unto the governor of the feast." The servants' thoughts were, "This is water, not wine. We should not serve this." However, the words of Jesus were to draw out and to serve. The servants looked to see which was right between their thoughts and the words of Jesus. They believed that the words of Jesus were right and followed them. This faith accomplished the miracle. Miraculous works are always formed in such conditions.

There was a man who had an infirmity for 38 years. Jesus said to him, "Rise, take up thy bed, and walk." This ill man thought, "I cannot walk. How can I take up my bed and walk when I can't even move? But Jesus is telling me to walk. Then am I right, or is Jesus right? Of course Jesus is. Then let me follow Jesus' words." Then, when he moved, the works of him taking up his bed and walking arose within him.

When Peter first met Jesus at the Sea of Galilee, Peter had cast his net all night long but had not caught a single fish. In the morning Jesus said to him, "Cast the net into the deep." Peter thought about this: "Cast the net into the deep? What fish are in the deep? There are no fish there. That is what my thoughts say, but Jesus is saying that there are fish. Then let me throw my thoughts away and follow the words of Jesus." Then Peter cast the net into the deep end and ended up catching so many fish that his net almost burst.

When I meet demon possessed people from time to time I

shout before the demon. "Demon! I am not going to fight against you! Why would I fight with you? I'm going to tell Jesus to fight for me. Can you beat Jesus?" I do not fight against the demon, but I pit Jesus to fight against him. Then Jesus defeats him.

I cannot break my thoughts. Can you break your thoughts? I have lived by my thoughts and have always believed that my thoughts were correct. But one day, I came to believe in Jesus. When I leave my thoughts as they are, those thoughts reign, but after receiving Jesus, I pit Him against my thoughts.

"My thoughts are like this, but what does the Lord say?"

When I pit the words of the Lord against my thoughts, the heart, "No matter how correct my thoughts seem, the words of the Lord are correct. I am wrong. The Word is right," arose in me so that my thoughts become powerless. The words of the Lord then led me. Each time this happened, I could experience the works of the power of God arising.

## When Colliding Against the Word of God

Abraham had his own thoughts: "How can I have a son? I am this old, and it has ceased to be with Sarah after the manner of women. . . ."

In the heart of God Abraham had a son, but in Abraham's thoughts and in Abraham's heart there was no son. Then whose thoughts are correct? There is no one among you who thinks that your thoughts are more correct than God's. People think that God's words are all correct. But the problem is you separate your thoughts from the Word of God and that is why you flow to your thoughts. You must pit the Word of God against your thoughts. Then the Word of God wins. There is no need for you to fight to defeat your thoughts.

People's hearts are bound to be led by circumstances. As I, too, grew older my memory weakened. I am sure I know a certain thing, but it does not come to mind at times. I cannot remember the names of people who I am close to. My vision has become weaker as well. A little while ago, I went to South America. After the service in Peru, the brothers and sisters wanted to take a picture together and we did. However, after a couple of flashes, I could not see. I regretfully asked them to take more pictures in the daytime. Nowadays, unless it's absolutely necessary, I try not to take pictures that require flash. I can't do anything about becoming older, memory loss, weakening vision, my body becoming weaker. . . . Before, I felt nothing although I drove all day long. But now I cannot do that.

Abraham was 99 years old, so how do you think he felt? "Me, have a son?" It must have seemed like a joke to him. Sarah, too, was an old woman. I often say that I would be afraid that such an old woman would have a child. Even if she did become pregnant, how could she give birth? That is why people naturally think that such a woman cannot have a child.

"God said that He would give us a son but we are so old. How could we have child?"

These thoughts are very natural to us. But when colliding against the Word of God, these thoughts are not higher than the Word of God and thus, must be denied before the word. In your eyes, it seems that you can not have a son, but when God says that you will, and when your thoughts differ from the

Word of God, you must select the Word of God. The problem is that you do not remember the Word of God and erase it from your hearts. When you lay your thoughts against the Word of God you can see that the Word of God is correct.

## Being Justified

This is also true with you receiving the forgiveness of sins. Jesus was crucified for your sins and He bore your sins. But you sin every day.

"I am a sinner. I sinned yesterday, and I am a sinner who sins even today. Jesus was crucified, but I am a sinner who cannot live without sinning."

"I have committed filthy, dirty, deceitful sins. I have many sins that are shameful to speak of. I have lived hiding those sins. That's the kind of person I am and how can I say that I have no sins? I am a sinner."

Those are your own thoughts. If this is true, what does the Word of God say? Whatever the Word of God says is correct. There is no way how you judge could ever be correct.

One day, I was reading 1 Corinthians chapter 6 and was completely shocked.

*Nor thieves, nor covetous, nor drunkards, nor revilers, nor extortioners, shall inherit the kingdom of God.* (1 Corinthians 6:10)

*And such were some of you: but ye are washed, but ye are sanctified, but ye are justified in the name of the Lord Jesus, and by the Spirit of our God.* (1 Corinthians 6:11)

The Bible says, ". . . and such were some of you." You committed the sins of stealing, being covetous, being drunk, and being extortionists. However, afterwards it says, ". . . but ye are washed, ye are sanctified, but ye are justified in the name of the Lord Jesus, and by the Spirit of our God." You had clearly sinned, but the Bible says that you have been cleansed, you have been sanctified, and you have been justified. Here, let us not believe only in our thoughts, but pit them against the Word of God. I am a dirty sinner in my thoughts, but the Word of God says, "You did commit those sins. But you are washed, sanctified, and justified inside the name of the Lord Jesus Christ and the Holy Spirit of God." Now, will you believe in your thoughts or the Word of God?

After receiving salvation, it seemed that all the other brothers and sisters changed when I heard their testimonies, but it seemed that I had not changed at all. It seemed there was no answer to my prayers, there was no one receiving salvation even though I witnessed, and there were no works of God. Those were my thoughts. What does the Bible say about this?

*Therefore if any man be in Christ, he is a new creature: old things are passed away; behold, all things are become new.* (2 Corinthians 5:17)

All things have become new and you have become a new person. How God sees and how I see differs. Is my view correct, or is God's? "In my eyes nothing has changed, but God says that I am changed. Then I am changed." That is what I believed.

You often hold only to your thoughts. You do not pit them against the Word of God, but just leave them, and thus, your own thoughts take hold of you. However, when those thoughts collide against the Word of God, the Word of God crumbles your thoughts and they are all destroyed.

## Search Within the Word of God

Abraham thought that he could not have a son until he faced the Word of God. God said, "Is anything too hard for the Lord? Your wife, Sarah, will surely bear you a son and you shall call his name Isaac." When these words came upon Abraham and he no longer stubbornly exerted his thoughts: "God said that He would give me a son. I do not think I can have a son. Then whose thoughts are correct? Of course God's words are right. Then let me believe in God." Abraham threw his thoughts away and believed the Word of God.

From time to time, you have your thoughts, but let not your thoughts be the end.

"This is what I think, but what does the Bible say?" When you pit your thoughts against the Word of God, the Word of God will prevail and your thoughts are broken. When your thoughts break and the Word of God is alive in you, the works of God begin from then on. This is called the, "works of faith."

*Through faith also Sara herself received strength to conceive seed. . . .* (Hebrews 11:11)

Sarah gained the strength to conceive when she believed. Faith does not come from nothing. Faith arises when the word enters you. Loving folks, do you want to have the faith of forgiveness of sins? Do you want assurance? Do you want to become born again? Do not search within your thoughts but search inside the Word of God. In your thoughts, you are a sinner who has sinned, but see what the Word of God has recorded. Then no matter how you think, believe that your sins are washed away if the Word of God says they are because the Word of God is higher than your thoughts. All people such as these are people of faith. When the Word of God reigns in you, the works of the power of God arise in your lives. I hope that through faith in the word, all of you will gain the assurance of the forgiveness of sins.

# 32

## *Cast Ishmael Out*

*And the child grew, and was weaned: and Abraham made a great feast the same day that Isaac was weaned. And Sarah saw the son of Hagar the Egyptian, which she had born unto Abraham, mocking. Wherefore she said unto Abraham, Cast out this bondwoman and her son: for the son of this bondwoman shall not be heir with my son, even with Isaac. And the thing was very grievous in Abraham's sight because of his son. And God said unto Abraham, Let it not be grievous in thy sight because of the lad, and because of thy bondwoman; in all that Sarah hath said unto thee, hearken unto her voice; for in Isaac shall thy seed be called.* (Genesis 21:8-12)

## He Probably Loves Ishmael.
## Why Did He Say to Cast Him Out?

There were two sons in the house of Abraham. One was Ishmael, who was borne through humanistic methods, and one was Isaac, who was borne through the faith to believe in God. These two sons grew up in the same home. Since the son who was borne following the flesh was much older than the son borne through the promise, Ishmael mocked Isaac whenever he had the chance. Sarah, upon seeing Isaac being mocked, tells Abraham, "Cast out this bondwoman and her son."

Abraham was the father of faith, yet he had many humanistic thoughts.

"Although Ishmael was born of distrust as a result of me having no faith, he still is my son. . . ."

Ishmael was already grown and Abraham had great expectations in him. Abraham had no intentions of casting Ishmael out. He was thus deeply worried when he heard Sarah's words. However, God told Abraham to cast this son out as well.

Long ago, I used to wonder, "How could merciful God say such a thing? Ishmael is also a son of Abraham and God must love Ishmael as well. Why did He say to cast him out?" I just could not understand it. There are many parts of the Bible that we do not understand. But after some time, we come to know that God accepts nothing done through the methods of man and only accepts the things accomplished through God, having come from the heart of God.

A story similar to this is the story of Cain and Abel's offerings. Abel offered the firstling of the flock and the fat thereof to God. Abel did not know how to give the offering and wanted to gain the heart of God. "I wonder what offering pleases God." Abel asked and sought of God, and came to know that the firstling of the flock and the fat thereof is the offering that pleased God.

Cain was not so. The crops and fruits from his farming looked so desirable that he offered them to God. This was Cain's heart, but was not something that pleased God. The "fruits of the ground" Cain offered refer to the fruits of the cursed earth, but also represents the product of the thought of man. It means that God cannot accept the fruits of the ground that come from the flesh.

Though they may be things not of faith in God, there are things in our lives that seem to a certain extent good, honest, and holy in the eyes of man. People, for the most part, trust in this.

"He is such a good person." "That person is so good he needs no laws." "He is such a moral person." "That person is so godly."

But God has never said this. This is the difference between God and man. God said, *The heart is deceitful above all things and desperately wicked.* (Jeremiah 17:9) God said that good does not dwell inside man. It is completely different from our thoughts.

## You Must Choose One or the Other

Abraham took a handmaid and bore a child of distrust. Even so, Ishmael was held in high hopes by Abraham because he had grown so much. God, however, said for Abraham to cast out this bondwoman and her son. This means that God will not accept things accomplished by the methods of man. That which you have done honestly and good, as well as the thanks you have given from your heart, God does not accept. God accepts the things that emanate from God, which are the things that come from the heart of God.

There are two ways to receive the forgiveness of sins. There is the way of receiving it through repenting of yourself, praying zealously, and being loyal to God. There also is the way of receiving forgiveness through the crucifixion of Jesus. Both of these ways cannot be chosen. Humanistic methods must be done away with if forgiveness is to be gained through the faith to believe in God. On the other hand, everything Jesus has done must be thrown away if you are to receive forgiveness through your effort and zeal. Only one of the two can be chosen. Both cannot.

The Bible tells us that God rejects everything that comes from man. Abraham was the father of faith, but placed hope in

Ishmael. He thought, "Ishmael is growing so well and he will lead our family well from now on." However, God told him to cast Ishmael out.

As I read these verses I truly felt that I was like Abraham. In the past, when I did not have the faith to believe in God I said, "Since I went to church this Sunday, God will happily receive me. Since I tithed; since I showed compassion to a beggar; since I did church work; since I gave all-night prayers; since I repented; since I fasted and prayed. . . ." I put all my expectations in and upon myself. I did not want to receive what Jesus accomplished, but placed my hope in my accomplishments. Nevertheless, as God spoke to Abraham, God was telling me to throw away everything I did through my methods. He was telling me that they were all useless.

## Alchemists, Who Tried to Make Gold

There were the alchemists during the Middle Ages. They tried to make gold by mixing copper and zinc. One day, when they came up with brass, the color was similar to gold and they rejoiced. They said, "If we experiment a bit more we can make gold!" and many alchemists experimented, trying to make gold. They sold their houses, land, and borrowed money to come up with funds for experiments in their efforts to make gold. However, they all ended in failure. As time passed and as their knowledge increased, people came to know that gold is an element. They discovered that since gold is an element, it cannot be made through mixing metals. Afterwards, people quit trying to make gold and there is no one today who tries to make gold.

They can make metals similar to gold, but no one can make gold. Likewise, holiness and righteousness are things that belong to God and must come from God. You cannot become holy or righteous through your labor and effort. Regardless of this, however, just as the alchemists tried to make gold, many people today try to accomplish spiritual life through their effort, laboring to become righteous and holy. Just as the alchemists thought making gold was possible when they came up with something similar to gold in their experiments, many people today think that they can become righteous because they see that at times their ambitions and greed have been calmed when they fast and try not to sin.

"Now I will reach the level of righteousness God requests! I will become holy! This is what Apostle Paul must have been like!" Actually, this was only a temporary shortness in lust due to fasting. Because one cannot continue going hungry, he starts eating, and the evil and lustful heart arises once again. Nothing has changed. Even so, people think, "This was just a bad ending. Let me begin again." Again he fasts, reads the Bible, and tries to become righteous.

I, too, have attempted this many times. When I fasted the sinful heart would disappear, but would come back to life after I had eaten. It is because, by nature, the flesh is ultimately filthy and dirty. God knows that we cannot become righteous through trimming and bettering the flesh. That is why He tells us to throw away everything that is of the flesh. Therefore, I threw away from my heart all the fasting prayers I had prayed. Sadly, some people keep the good they have done as crowns in their heart.

"I fasted for 40 days."

"I read the New Testament 100 times."

"I have never missed a Sunday service."

But in the eyes of God, a person who has never missed Sunday service or a person who has never attended a service are the same sinners. We are righteous when Jesus comes into us. Everything that proceeds from man is the same.

Among ants there are those with thick legs and those with thin ones. Some ants boast that they have thick legs and some boast that they are good looking, saying, "I am Miss Ant." However, in the eyes of man, this ant and that ant are all the same. A turtle that wins a gold medal for sprinting at the Turtle Olympics is still nothing but slow in the eyes of man.

You may be clean in your own eyes or in the eyes of your neighbors. You may also be truthful. You may even be honest. But in the eyes of God, we are all the same dirty humans. God has already crossed us out.

*There is none righteous, no, not one. . . .* (Romans 3:10)

## If Not Exposed, It Loses the Opportunity to Be Cured

Because man cannot become righteous on his own, God sent Jesus Christ. We put Jesus aside, however, and try to become good, holy, and truthful ourselves. We try ourselves to not sin. To a certain extent, it seems as if it is working and people put their hopes there. But this should not work. It is a problem when it goes well. Even during the time of Jesus, it was the harlots, publicans, and people like the woman caught in the act of adultery who received the grace of Jesus. The scribes and Pharisees who thought they did well all went against Jesus.

A wild olive tree should bear wild olives. If it bears good olives, this is a serious problem. We dirty, filthy, and evil humans should bear wickedness and commit sins. If we dirty humans do good, it is a problem. We should be dirty. There can be only one who is good, and that is God. Therefore, you must first discover that there is no good in you in order for you to have true faith.

God told Abraham to cast Ishmael and the handmaid out. Why did God say this when Ishmael is also Abraham's son? It was because he was of the flesh. Just as God said this to Abraham, God tells you to throw away everything that is of man. You may not want to throw it away but keep everything, but they should be thrown away.

If you have good works such as, "I built a chapel. I established a church. I gave a large offering and was in charge of the church finances. I fasted for 40 days. I have never withheld tithes. I did not sin," such things cover your sinful nature. It keeps your sinful nature from being revealed and distracts you from receiving salvation. If you are a dirty human being, your dirty nature should be revealed in order for you to be saved. However, it is a problem when this is not revealed and only the cleaner things are. A person with cancer should have his cancer revealed; someone with leprosy should have his leprosy revealed; and someone with tuberculosis should have his tuberculosis revealed to have the opportunity to have the disease cured. If the disease is not revealed, it is like someone dying without knowing the reason and losing his opportunity to be healed.

We should not be good. If God says that we are evil, then we should be evil. When there is no good in you and the evil is revealed and you say, "Ah, a body of death I am! I am sick of this man! This dirty man!" giving up on yourself, you can accept Jesus. However, Satan constantly tries to reveal goodness in us and deceives us into thinking there actually is some good within us. This keeps us from going to the side of the faith in God and makes you put expectations in yourself.

## Throw Everything Away and Turn to Jesus

Abraham was content with Isaac, but also put much expectation in Ishmael. God told Ishmael to be cast out. This is also true with us. We have many things we received when we relied on God, but we also have many things derived from the goodness we have done, the kindness we have bestowed, and the compassion we have given to others. These things become a distraction to our spiritual life and keep us from accepting true salvation. Because people do not know this, there are so many people who are deceived by this and proudly boast of what they have done. Such people cannot receive the grace of God.

The Bible tells us to coldly cast this flesh of ours out. It is because we lose the opportunity to receive the grace of God unless we throw this away. I was a truly dirty, evil human being but the little good I had done, having gone to church, and having gone to early morning services became my own righteousness, covering my sins, and I almost did not receive salvation. Thankfully, one day God lent me His eyes. For the first time I saw myself through the eyes of God. I saw myself till that day as an okay, faithful, and honest person, but my image in the eyes of God was so dirty and filthy.

Right then I believed the Word of God.

*The heart is deceitful above all things and desperately wicked.* (Jeremiah 17:9)

This is when I discovered that there is no good, righteousness, or holiness inside of me. I then naturally began to give up on myself. I came to distrust myself. When I realized that I was a dirty human and that I could do nothing, all my expectations of receiving salvation through my good deeds fell apart. When that expectation fell apart, I was able to receive the grace of Jesus. Since I was now saved by the grace of Jesus, it did not matter what good I did or did not do.

I once was attempting to travel somewhere by car, but my car was broken down so I had to ride in my friend's car. Therefore, the fact that my car was broken would have nothing to do with me getting there. Whether my car had a flat tire, whether the ignition did not turn on, or whether the engine was broken, none of those things mattered. I can leave it behind and ride in my friend's car.

I left everything of me behind and am riding in Jesus' car. Now, my evil and filthiness are not problems anymore. I am strengthened by the righteousness of Jesus, and strengthened by the power of Jesus. Because the holiness of Jesus comes to me and sanctifies me, whether I do well or not has nothing to do with my sanctification.

## Cast Out Everything Done by the Efforts of Man

Salvation cannot be achieved through your own goodness. It is achieved through Jesus. Therefore, our works are not necessary. It must completely be through Jesus. If you rely on your goodness, your works, and your efforts, you can never be saved. And God, to have us realize this, told Abraham to cast out Ishmael. He is telling us to cast out everything done through man.

Loving folks, you must throw away all the good you have done in order for you to receive the grace of God, because with it, you can never stand before God. Those things may appear precious and beautiful in your eyes, but they keep you from being able to stand before God. We are humans who can only be cursed and destroyed. Only the blood Jesus Christ shed on the cross has cleansed us. We are, by nature, dirty humans and we can only go to heaven through the grace of the cross. We need to have this faith and must deny all the good we have done. When we deny the good we have done, true faith comes upon us and the grace of salvation accomplished at the cross reaches us.

# 33

# *Abraham Who Offered Isaac by Faith*

*And it came to pass after these things, that God did tempt Abraham, and said unto him, Abraham: and he said, Behold, here I am. And he said, Take now thy son, thine only son Isaac, whom thou lovest, and get thee into the land of Moriah; and offer him there for a burnt offering upon one of the mountains which I will tell thee of. And Abraham rose up early in the morning, and saddled his ass, and took two of his young men with him, and Isaac his son, and clave the wood for the burnt offering, and rose up, and went unto the place of which God had told him. Then on the third day Abraham lifted up his eyes, and saw the place afar off.* (Genesis 22:1-4)

## The Change That Opened My Covered Heart

There were many changes I experienced in my life after receiving salvation. One of them was how God had me open my heart. Before, I would not trust other people's words, and I also did not speak straight from my heart. I thought telling everything that was in my heart would be foolish and idiotic because others then would be able to see everything inside of me. I thought a person was wise when saying things different from what was in his heart. In this manner, I had never opened my heart to another person.

Another reason I did not open my heart was that I wanted to make myself look great in front of others. If I were to speak honestly, my shortcomings would be revealed and I did not like that. Therefore people did not know my heart, as I had not once opened my heart and had a conversation because I wanted to amplify myself as a good person. I would only answer according to what the circumstances were. I would only listen to others with my ears, but I had never accepted their words with my heart.

Even when listening to the Word of God, I would say, "That's what the Word of God says, but this is what I think," and did not accept the words for what they were. I only followed my thoughts and my perceptions. One day, however, I became startled as I was reading the Word of God. "Surely I had lived like a fool!"

My opinions were so foolish, stupid, and pitiful compared to the heart and the will of God. In addition, I realized how foolish it was to follow my thoughts without accepting the words that stated that God knows everything regarding my future and that He is working for me.

My heart crumbled down from that moment on and the words of God began to enter my heart, one by one. Before, I had myself established at the core of my heart and accepted only the words that fit me or looked right in my eyes. But now, regardless of what words I receive from God, though they may appear to not fit my heart or appear incorrect, I think, "Are my thoughts right or is the Word of God right?" and throw my thoughts away more and more.

The interesting thing is that as I began to accept the words of God, I was able to accept the words of people as well. I was able to accept my wife's words into my heart, my children's words, and even accept the words of my colleagues and church members into my heart. As I accepted other people's words into my heart, their hearts and mine would become one, and I was able to be completely free and have much peace. I often thought, "Why did I not live in this kind of a wonderful world earlier on?"

## The Taste of Man Apart from Faith

I came to know that Abraham went through the same kind of change that I had. God called Abraham in Genesis chapter 12 and said:

*. . . Get thee out of thy country, and from thy kindred, and from thy father's house, unto a land that I will shew thee: And I will make of thee a great nation, and I will bless thee, and make thy name great; and thou shalt be a blessing:* (Genesis 12:1-2)

Abraham followed these words of promise, leaving his country, his father's house, and going to the land of Canaan. However, a famine hit the land as soon as he arrived at Canaan, so he went down to Egypt. As he went, he thought, "My wife is so beautiful that the people of Egypt may try to take my wife from me and kill me." He told his wife, "Call me your brother and say that you are my sister."

Because God said to Abraham, "I will make of thee a great nation, and I will make you into a blessing," Abraham, therefore, cannot die. But Abraham did not have faith that God would protect him in order to keep His promise. The promise God made to him was not in his heart and only his thoughts remained. Thus, he thought, "The Egyptians may kill me to take my wife. I should say that she is my sister in order to protect my life."

These kinds of thoughts are possible only apart from the faith to trust in the promise of God. The ingredients of the foods determine the flavors of the foods. Likewise, people with faith have the flavor of faith. People who have the Word of God in their hearts have unique thoughts that are made only through the Word. Just as you can get an egg if you raise a hen, there is a unique power, beauty, love and peace that come about from the word when faith enters your heart.

Had the Word of God been alive in Abraham's heart, he would have thought, "No, God said that He will make me into a great nation. How can that happen if I die?" when he felt that the Egyptians were going to kill him and take his wife. He would have immediately been freed from his worries and fears. The thoughts that arise from having the word alive in your heart cannot be imitated or produced through anything else.

Even after this incident, Abraham continued to have no faith, and when he could not have a child with his wife Sarah, he had Ishmael by taking his wife's handmaid. Had there been the slightest possibility that Abraham's wife, Sarah, could have a son, would she have sent another woman into her husband's room? When we analyze Sarah's heart about the time she gave Hagar to Abraham as a concubine, we can see that such a thought is only possible when she was absolutely sure that she could not have a son. What kind of a woman would want to allow her husband to be with another woman? Although God had said that He would give her a son, she had the heart that she could not have a son, which was a heart formed from distrust.

You may sing hymns, pray, read the Bible, or witness, but the thoughts and life that come about through having faith in one's heart cannot be imitated. A person with faith and a person without are completely different when it comes to certain things.

## If the Word Is Alive in Your Heart

Suppose I wanted to go to the United States with my son. I say to him, "We will be going to America and I purchased your airplane ticket. So you just pack your bags and come along." If he trusts my words, he would be completely free concerning the airplane ticket, no matter how expensive or difficult it is to obtain. If my son is worried about the airplane tickets, it comes forth from distrusting my words.

The faith to receive salvation from sin works in the exact same way. This is what God has said:

*I have blotted out, as a thick cloud, thy transgressions, and, as a cloud, thy sins: return unto me; for I have redeemed thee.* (Isaiah 44:22)

*But he was wounded for our transgressions, he was bruised for our iniquities: the chastisement of our peace was upon him; and with his stripes we are healed. All we like sheep have gone astray; we have turned every one to his own way; and the LORD hath laid on him the iniquity of us all.* (Isaiah 53:5-6)

If these words are alive in your heart, these words defeat all thoughts of sin. Even if the thoughts, "I sinned today; I committed evil today; I have many sins . . . ," arise in you, these words immediately stir up in your heart, "God said that He laid all of our sins upon Jesus, and Jesus bore them. These sins are taken care of." The word defeats all fears of sin when the word is alive in your heart.

Although God said to Abraham, "I will make of thee a great nation," he was afraid that he would be killed. It wasn't that this fear defeated the Word of God, but rather, the fear was working in his heart because he had no faith to believe in the word in his heart. If you have the faith to trust in the Word of God, there is nothing that can defeat it. Regardless of what circumstance you are in, the things of the present, nor the things of the future, nor powers, nor height, nor depth, nor whatever it is that you face, it cannot erase the Word of God from inside you.

## Yes, It Can Be Done if God Does It!

Much time had passed, and God once again appeared to Abraham when he was 99 years old.

"You shall not be called Abram, but be called Abraham. I will make you into a great nation. I will have your wife deliver you a son."

Abraham laughed.

"How could someone who's one hundred years old have a son? Sarah is ninety."

God once again spoke to Abraham, "No, your wife, Sarah, will surely bear you a son. Thou shalt call his name Isaac."

Right then Abraham realized that he had distrusted God. He said, "Right, it can be done if God does it!" and was able to have faith in his heart.

"Then I will have a son! If God gives me a son, although my wife and I are old, we will have a son!"

When he had that faith, God gave Abraham a son.

Before, Abraham would accept the Word of God within his limitations and calculations. But Abraham now had the faith that it can indeed be done if God does it because God is almighty. God taught that faith to Abraham, and Abraham learned this faith and had a son.

## Offer Isaac as a Burnt Offering

Abraham's son, Isaac, grew much. Then one day, God spoke to Abraham, "Take thy only son, Isaac, to Mt. Moriah which I have told you of and offer him as a burnt offering."

A burnt offering involves skinning a sheep or a cow, cutting it into pieces, removing all its intestines, washing them out in water, and burning it in the fire. However, God was telling Abraham to give not a cow or a sheep, but Isaac as a burnt offering. What kind of a heart do you think Abraham had then?

God promised Abraham, "You will have many seeds like the stars in the sky and the sands of the sea through Isaac." He also promised, "Christ, who will have all mankind be blessed, will be born through Isaac," and Abraham believed this promise. Therefore, when God said to offer Isaac, the faith, "How could the promise of God be achieved if Isaac dies? Ah, even if I do give him as a burnt offering, God will bring him to life to fulfill His promise! Even if I kill Isaac he will come to life, be married, have a son, and have many descendants like the stars of the sky and the sands of the sea. And Christ will be born among his descendants!" arose in his heart. Thus, freedom came upon Abraham's heart.

Abraham then placed some wood, which is the first thing necessary for the burnt offering, upon Isaac's back and led Isaac to Mt. Moriah. Then at the peak of the mountain, he tied Isaac onto the altar and was going to kill him with a knife. If Abraham did not have the faith to believe in the promise of

God, he would have said, "Isaac, today is your last day. I have to kill you with my own hands today. I don't know why it is so hard to believe in God. Isaac, do not hate your father for this." He would be in unbearable agony, despair, and a heartbreaking pain. He might have said, "God, I will die instead. I can never offer Isaac. How could I kill the son I gained at the age of 100? God, forgive me. I cannot do this." All kinds of thoughts would have risen from Abraham's heart.

However, when we read the Bible, Abraham was not that way. In Hebrews chapter 11, it says that Abraham offered Isaac through faith.

*By faith . . . Abraham . . . offered up Isaac . . . Of whom it was said, That IN ISAAC SHALL THY SEED BE CALLED: Accounting that God was able to raise him up, even from the dead; from whence also he received him in a figure.* (Hebrews 11:17-19)

Abraham was neither afraid nor sad because he had faith. He had the heart, "Now I will see the power of God. I will see how God brings him back to life when I kill Isaac." Then he tried to kill Isaac with a knife to offer him as a burnt offering. Right then God said, "Abraham! Abraham!" and told him not to lay his hand on Isaac. "God, I will kill him. Didn't you tell me to kill him?" Isaac was no longer something for Abraham to worry about, but for God.

## Not Knowing the Heart of God Who Had Jesus Crucified

People without faith are unable to believe in God and try to do the things God should do. How painful and miserable it would be if Abraham was told to kill Isaac when he had no faith! When you do not have faith, everything becomes your responsibility. It becomes your responsibility to wash your sins away, to keep from committing sins, and to live happily. However, if you have the faith to believe in God, then all of these things are no longer yours but God's.

Faith is God's heart and your heart becoming one. When what you are trying to do is what God is trying to do, there is nothing to worry about. Because it was God's work to establish Isaac in order for Christ, who would save all of mankind, to be born, Abraham has nothing to worry about in protecting Isaac.

There are many people who are suffering because they have not received the forgiveness of sin. Why do they live this way? It is because they are trying to wash their sins away themselves. It is because they do not know the heart of God that wants to wash their sins away and the heart of God that did not spare His only begotten son, but crucified Him. When we see Jesus who was crucified, we can discover the will of God that wanted to wash our sins away. If God wanted to wash our sins away, why could He not wash away our sins? But people are unable to understand and accept the heart of God that is for us and simply fall into thinking, "I have to wash my sins away," and labor to somehow wash them away.

If you were to take care of your sins, what means do you possess to go about doing so? If we could take care of our sins, why would Jesus have to be crucified and killed? Because we cannot do it, God sent His son, Jesus Christ, to be crucified. God sent His son to this earth and had Him crucified to wash our sins away. Then could that not wash our sins away? We must search for the answer to this inside the Scriptures.

Nevertheless, people do not open the Bible to see whether the death of Jesus washed their sins away or not. There are so many people who simply ignore God and follow their own thoughts.

## If You Become a Person Who Believes the Promise

Abraham first lived without faith. He did not value or believe the word and followed his own thoughts although he did hear the word. Even though God said that He would make him into a great nation, he strained to save himself. When it seemed in his thoughts that he could not have a son, he took a handmaid and had a son. Abraham, who was like this, gained faith to believe in God as he walked with God. Afterwards, when it was time for Isaac to be married, he sent his old servant, saying, "God promised me. He said that He will give me many seeds through Isaac. A wife for Isaac has been prepared."

The faith to believe in God came upon Abraham. Therefore, he was able to cast all of his burdens upon God, and was truly at peace. Suppose Abraham had to labor to gain many seeds like the stars of the sky and sands of the sea. How difficult it would be! He would always be anxious, thinking, "Isaac should quickly have children. Why isn't he having children?"

Our receiving the forgiveness of sins, living the holy life, or living the bright life, all of these things are God's responsibilities. But when we do not have the faith to believe this, we try to do these things ourselves and we labor. If you become people with faith in God, however, true peace will come upon you and God will add His grace to your lives.

# 34

# *Abraham Who Read God's Heart*

*And the angel of the LORD called unto Abraham out of heaven the second time, And said, By myself have I sworn, saith the LORD, for because thou hast done this thing, and hast not withheld thy son, thine only son: That in blessing I will bless thee, and in multiplying I will multiply thy seed as the stars of the heaven, and as the sand which is upon the sea shore; and thy seed shall possess the gate of his enemies; And in thy seed shall all the nations of the earth be blessed; because thou hast obeyed my voice.* (Genesis 22:15-18)

## Peace Brought by Faith

Spiritual life is extremely easy and peaceful. I was able to put all the worries of my heart to sleep as long as I was living the spiritual life of believing in God. I was especially able to defeat insecurity and fear through the faith to believe in the promise of God. Since I am a pastor, people may think, "Pastor Park must be godly," but when I look at myself I am truly a lacking and pitiful person before God. Fleshly things and evil thoughts always arise in my heart. Before, when such hearts would arise, I would say to myself, "I should not have these kinds of hearts. I, I should not be like this!" and fall into fear and worry. Now, however, I am no longer that way. Because God saved me, having known me and made me His servant, He takes the responsibility for everything about me. My sins and blemishes are not my problems, but God's. I have so much peace in my heart because it is not I who am trying to repair all such things, but I believe that it is God who repairs them.

God said, "Take now thy son, thine only son Isaac, whom

thou lovest, and get thee into the land of Mt. Moriah and offer him as a burnt offering," to Abraham in Genesis chapter 22. If people were to hear such a voice and offer their son, how painful it would be! But that was not the case with Abraham because he had faith to believe in God. Spiritual life became so easy for Abraham after he came to know and believe the heart of God.

## Upon Seeing Myself in the Eyes of God

I had not known myself well. Although I was living a filthy, evil, and deceitful life, when I thought of myself using my standard, I was still a clean person, a person with a good spiritual life, a smart person, and a great person. One day, God bestowed grace upon me, who had once thought this way. I think God let me borrow His eyes. The eyes to see myself from an angle completely different from my own were opened. Right then I was truly amazed because I discovered there was no one as filthy, dirty, or evil as I was and there was no one as foolish and deceitful as I was. The heart to honor myself came crumbling down upon seeing this.

Before, "I" was the standard of everything because I had myself firmly established. I would accept whatever appeared good and correct in my heart, and I did not accept anything else. I knew the Word of God because I had heard it before, but I had not accepted it into my heart. I had much knowledge of the Bible, but not even the slightest bit of the heart of God remained in my heart. Thus, I had to be afraid, insecure, and ashamed. I lived a life of having no rest in my heart.

One day, I came to see myself as seen through the eyes of God.

*The heart is deceitful above all things and desperately wicked: who can know it?* (Jeremiah 17:9)

My heart as seen through the eyes of God is deceitful and desperately wicked. However, my heart seen through my eyes was not so. I would say, "Though I lie some, though I have some darkness, I am still good." I lived both my physical life and my spiritual life having a standard completely different from God. But when I saw myself as seen by God, I came to discover that I was a dirty and evil man who deserved to be cursed and destroyed. I became disillusioned toward myself and I began to hate myself. I would look in the mirror and shout, "Ock Soo Park! You filthy man, you deceitful wretch!"

I began to change when the faith to trust in myself crumbled down. When my own heart would be standing firmly, I only accepted things that fit my heart, no matter what it was. But since my heart crumbled down, the Word of God, which did not fit my heart before, started to enter me and my life began to change completely and I became renewed.

## God, Give Us Water!

The Bible says that Noah received the grace of God. In other words, Noah found grace in the eyes of God. God clearly told Noah, "Wickedness is great in the earth and I will destroy them with water," while also telling him to, "Make thee an ark of gopher wood. . . ." Here Noah discovers the heart of God that is bestowing grace upon him. He then had the heart, "God wants to save me. God wants to bestow grace upon me. Then, I should make an ark." With the faith, "How will I build the ark? I don't know, but since God wants to save me, I only need to follow the Word of God!" Noah was able to build the ark.

I, too, came to know the heart of God while receiving the Word of God in my life. We built a retreat center on Mt. Daeduk, which is located in Gimcheon City. Water was difficult to come by because we had built it at the top of the mountain. We needed tremendous amounts of water in order for people to drink, wash, shower, prepare meals, and do the dishes during the retreat. We wanted to develop the ground water and we needed more than three hundred tons of water a day. We drilled 3,600 feet underground to find water, but when we found none, we were unspeakably disappointed.

"How can we hold retreats without water?"

I prayed to God early every morning.

"God, give us water!"

After I received salvation and Jesus entered my heart, I could feel from time to time the Lord leading me to His thoughts that were different from mine. When I had prayed about twenty days for this water problem, certain thoughts began to connect within me. When we bought the mountain where we built the retreat center, it was impossible, but we purchased it through the grace of God. Also, it seemed unlikely for us to be able to make a road up the mountain because of the village below, yet it was done through the help of God. And especially, I thought of how we laid a bridge over the creek at the entrance of the mountain. . . .

In building the bridge, large pilings had to be driven into the creek to withstand the bridge's load, which was costly. This was extremely difficult for us who had no construction experience. In addition, the people of the village claimed that building the bridge near their fields or farms would skew the water flow and damage their farming, causing a dispute as to where the bridge should be laid. Ultimately, a city hall officer said to build the bridge right above the waterfall to end the dispute and we ended up building the bridge further down from where we wanted to build it. Then at that place we tried to drive the large pilings, but the ground was solid rock. We did not have to drive pilings; we could construct the bridge right away. In the middle of the bridge construction, a city hall officer came out one day and asked us why we were doing the construction without driving pilings. When we told him that the ground was solid rock, he said that there could not be a solid rock in the creek and did not believe us. When a crane scraped the floor of the creek and revealed that it was indeed solid rock, the city hall officer shook his head, saying, "This is strange. . . . I've never seen such a thing in my life!" and left.

Because of the dispute among the villagers, we were able to move the bridge's location and conserve hundreds of thousands of dollars. We could see the help of God in this. Even after this, we often saw the hand of God helping in the construction of the retreat center. There were many things that were impossible unless God helped, and I could not deny it was God who did these things.

While I was praying for water, the many times God helped us came to mind, and I had the heart, "I helped you so much like this. Won't I help you in getting the water as well?" Even though we built the bridge and finished building the retreat center, we cannot hold a retreat unless we have water, and thus all of these would be useless. The retreat center also had a swimming pool for children.

We would receive eighty tons of water a day from that creek and save the water in a tank and use it little by little, but this was far from enough as we had many events and more people were coming. So we dug in search of ground water. The construction began and I had hopes of a hot spring. But far from hot springs, even regular water was nowhere to be found. We drilled through underground bedrock with a machine. Rather than having water spring forth, white smoke-like rock powder sprang up from the pipes, covering the mountain with powder, making it look like there was a fire on the mountain. It felt as though my heart was burning away. When we drilled 3,600 feet deep and there was no water, I prayed to God and He spoke to my heart.

"I helped you when you bought the mountain. I helped you during the building of the bridge, the road, when paving the road; in getting the permit to cut down the trees, I helped you, and in building the retreat center, in getting the electricity and telephone, I helped you."

If God does not help me with the final problem, the water problem, all the help I had received till now were meaningless. When God made me think about this, the heart that God would give us water arose within me.

## You Can Never Get Water Here

Before this, we called an underground water doctor. It costs ten thousand dollars to have him search for a day, but we agreed to have him for only a half a day for five thousand dollars. He came and saw where we had dug for a spring. He then asked, "Who said to dig here?"

"We just dug here."

"You can never get water here."

"Sir, we know that we cannot get water here. Tell us where we can get water." He looked over the mountain and said, "You cannot get water from this mountain." Then he got in his car, drove about 3.5 kilometers down toward the entrance of the village, and told us to drill there because there is water there. Even if there is water there, how could we draw that water to the retreat center at the top of the mountain? I was very disappointed.

But as I prayed to God, the faith that God would surely give us water constantly arose in my heart. So I gave a testimony at church while preaching.

"We spent over $100,000 to drill 3,600 feet underground but did not find a drop of water. The water doctor says that there is no water on that mountain, but God gave me the faith in my heart that He would give us water. Now God will give us water!"

I read the heart of God. "God was pleased with our holding retreats and helped in every aspect of the construction of the retreat center. Then He will give us water as well!" Then I forgot about the water problem.

Time passed, and one day during the retreat, there was an announcement saying, "Everyone, there is water left over so please use all you would like." I could not understand and called the brother who made the announcement.

"How could there be water left over?"

"Pastor, we have water left over."

I spoke with the brother who found the water. When the hole we had drilled for the ground water did not give us any, he had to fill that hole. If it does not become filled, dirty things would enter through the pipe and pollute the underground area. To fill this hole, he had to remove the pipes we had put in. But it was not easy removing pipes that were 3,600 feet deep. When he then hooked the pipes to a excavator and pulled, the excavator would be lifted while the pipes did not budge at all. Then the brother pushed and pulled the pipes with the excavator to remove them. Suddenly, "Pop!" and water came gushing out. The brothers were so happy, shouting, "There is water!" and sang and danced together. When they calculated the quantity of water, it was 450 tons of water a day.

## Because Abraham Read God's Heart

When I read the Bible, I don't read the contents but the heart of God. A few years ago when my son was studying abroad, I would once in a while tell my son, "Hey big guy, write me a letter once in a while." Then my son would send me a letter. Since it is a letter from my loving son, I would skim over it and leave it in my bag. Then later, when I have time, I would calmly pick it up and read it slowly. This time I am not only reading the contents but thinking, "I wonder why he is saying this," and trying to read my son's heart inside the letter.

When we read the Bible, only the storyline enters our eyes in the beginning. The story of how David killed Goliath with a sling and a stone and the story of Esther are very enjoyable. But when we read the Bible through receiving the heart of God, we can see God's heart inside the Bible.

Noah also read the heart of God.

"On one side of God's heart, He has the heart to save us, who should be destroyed for our sinfulness! God is trying to bestow grace on us to save us! Then we shall be saved!"

Noah could build the ark because he not only listened to the words of God but read God's heart.

In the beginning, Abraham only listened to the words of God but could not accept the heart of God who was saying those words. Therefore he always spoke of his own thoughts. But one day, Abraham read God's heart.

"Why is God telling me to leave my country, my kindred, and my father's house? The heart of God is to make me into a great nation. Then I will become a great nation. My seed will be many like the stars of the sky and the sands of the seashore."

God did much work upon Abraham and now Abraham is not only listening to the words of God but seeing the heart of God. Thus he was able to have that heart. He was now able to have the faith that God will give him a son. According to this faith he gained Isaac.

Even when God told Abraham to offer Isaac as a burnt offering on Mt. Moriah, Abraham knew the heart of God. Since he knows that through Isaac God will give him many seeds like the stars of the sky and the sands of the seashore, Abraham was so free.

"Sure, God did tell me to offer Isaac, but God will give me many seeds like the stars of the sky and the sands of the seashore through Isaac. Therefore, even if I do give him as an offering, he will ultimately live, marry, and have children."

This is how Abraham expressed his faith.

## Spiritual Life Is Reading God's Heart

Faith is reading God's heart. When I read the Bible after knowing the world of faith, each and every verse of the Scriptures were not mere stories, but I came to realize they were the heart of God. I changed when I received the heart of God through the words of the Bible into my heart as I read the Bible. Jesus was born in a filthy, dirty stable but it changed into a glorious place where the singing of the angels could be heard. Likewise, when the heart of God entered the dirty, filthy, and evil heart of mine, my heart became glorious. Now the heart of God was working inside me.

Abraham received the heart of God. Abraham knew God's heart, and God knew Abraham's heart. What did God say to Abraham?

"Seeing that thou hast not withheld thy son, thine only son from me. . . ."

God read the heart of Abraham who had not spared his only son through having faith in God. God read Abraham's heart and Abraham read God's heart. Through this, God's and Abraham's hearts became one. Their hearts united into one. From then on, Abraham was not worried no matter what he did. In Isaac's marriage or in having children, God would accomplish them all.

When I, too, discover that my heart is one with God's, I have true freedom and peace because I have faith that God will accomplish everything even if I do not step up to make it happen. Often, the things I faced seemed to be impossible; seemed to be big problems. But regardless of how they were in the eyes of man, I had confidence in my work because I had the heart that God would accomplish these things.

Loving folks, I am truly a filthy, dirty, and sinful human being, but I discovered God's heart of wanting to cleanse me. The will of God was to cleanse me, even if He had to send His son Jesus Christ to this earth. I read that will of God. Thus, through believing that God cleansed me of my sins, God and I became one and I had rest in my heart.

Spiritual life is reading God's heart. It is receiving God's heart. When God's heart and my heart become one, no matter what I do, it is accomplished by God, and I have rest and freedom and it brings glory to God. If you do not have the heart of God, your own thoughts will lead you. I hope that you will be freed from this, receive the heart of God, and become people who live with the same heart as God.

# 35

# *Freedom and Peace for Those with Faith*

*And Abraham was old, and well stricken in age: and the LORD had blessed Abraham in all things. And Abraham said unto his eldest servant of his house, that ruled over all that he had, Put, I pray thee, thy hand under my thigh: And I will make thee swear by the LORD, the God of heaven, and the God of the earth, that thou shalt not take a wife unto my son of the daughters of the Canaanites, among whom I dwell: But thou shalt go unto my country, and to my kindred, and take a wife unto my son Isaac. And the servant said unto him, Peradventure the woman will not be willing to follow me unto this land: must I needs bring thy son again unto the land from whence thou camest? And Abraham said unto him, Beware thou that thou bring not my son thither again. The LORD God of heaven, which took me from my father's house, and from the land of my kindred, and which spake unto me, and that sware unto me, saying, Unto thy seed will I give this land; he shall send his angel before thee, and thou shalt take a wife unto my son from thence.* (Genesis 24:1-7)

## The Two Opposing Lives

The Bible speaks to us of the world of faith. The life of a person who has faith is very different from a person who has no faith. There was no electricity at the house in which I lived in the Korean country side. Then when electricity came, our home became well lit and our lives had become completely changed. Once we had electricity, we could watch television, use a refrigerator, and turn on an air conditioner. Likewise, once I got a car, my life also changed very much; so much so, that my life afterwards could in no way be compared to my life before.

God is with us and Jesus is at our side. People with faith have Jesus in their hearts while those without faith do not have Jesus in theirs. In other words, though you may have a car, you cannot use it if you do not believe that you have one. Though you may have electricity, you cannot use it if you think you do not have it. Such people are without faith. Although God is there helping people like them, they do not try to solve their problems through God. They do not try to receive the grace and mercy of God, but try to do whatever it takes to accomplish things on their own. The unique characteristic of those who are without faith is they do not believe God will work, and labor on their own to do everything themselves.

In certain ways, Abraham was the same. God clearly promised Abraham, "I will make you into a great nation." When God promised this, if Abraham believed, saying, "God will give me many descendants," then he would have true freedom and peace. However, since he did not have faith, Abraham labored himself to have a son when he became old.

This was not only true with Abraham, but everyone's spiritual lives appear to be this way. For example, if you do not know the will and providence of God whose Son was crucified to forgive our sins, we strain ourselves to be freed from sin. Doing this, however, will not free us from sin, but we continue to do what we do only because we cannot believe that God will free us from sin.

When there were difficult problems, pains, or worries in my life, I did not have the power to take care of those problems, but I would have peace and rest when I obtained the faith that God is with me and takes care of those problems. God works when we look to God. The Bible says in Mark chapter 11, verse 24, *Therefore I say unto you, What things soever ye desire when ye pray, believe that ye receive them, and ye shall have them.* The Bible is clearly saying that if you believe that God will accomplish something, it shall be done. But since people do not have the faith that God will accomplish everything and since they feel that God will not, there are many people who are trying to accomplish these things themselves.

## The Point Where Abraham Changed

Up to a certain point, Abraham lived without faith in God. He did follow God concerning certain things and God did bless Abraham concerning those things. In addition, God did work upon Abraham, but it was at the age of 99 that Abraham was able to obtain true faith. God appeared unto Abraham when he was 99 and said, "Neither shall thy name any more be called Abram; but thy name shall be Abraham: for a father of many nations have I made thee." Then He said, "Your wife Sarah shall bear thee a son." At that very moment, when Abraham looked at himself, it seemed that there was no way he could have a son. In addition, his wife, Sarah, was old and it had ceased to be with her after the manner of women. Therefore, he felt that it would be even more difficult for his wife to have a child because she could not even have one when she was young. Therefore, Abraham laughed and answered, "O that Ishmael might live before thee!" In that instant, God fought with Abraham.

"No. Your wife Sarah shall surely give you a son and thou shalt call his name Isaac." When God said this twice, the heart of Abraham that till now could not believe he would have a child changed through hearing these words.

"This was my thought. But why won't I have a son if God allows me to? Since God said that I will surely have a son, God will give me a son!"

From then on Abraham's faith to believe in God changed. Before, he heard the Word of God upon the foundation of his own experience and knowledge. Now he was ignoring all of that and received the Word of God exactly as it was. When he had faith and his heart became one with the heart of God who said that a son would be given, the work of God started. We need this process as we live our spiritual life. There has to be that process of your own thoughts changing from the world of thought based on your own experience and living.

When time passed and Isaac was grown, God one day called Abraham to give Isaac for a burnt offering on Mt. Moriah. Before, he would have said, "How could I kill my loving son? I can't do that. . . ." But Abraham knew precisely the heart of God.

"Since He said that He would give me many descendants through Isaac, Isaac will ultimately live and have a son!"

Therefore Abraham did not hesitate in giving Isaac for a burnt offering. Abraham had the faith that even if he kills Isaac, burns him, and turns him into ashes, God will revive Isaac according to the promise of God, and provide many descendants like the stars of the sky and sands of the seashore through Isaac. Abraham knew precisely that it was God's work, not his, to have many descendants born through Isaac. Therefore, there was nothing for him to do, and he had much freedom and peace.

## The Old Servant's Conflict

More time passed and it was time for Isaac to marry. Abraham thought about this. Isaac had to be married in order for him to become a great nation. However, if a woman who cannot have a child marries into the family, it would not be a problem because God would make it so they would have a son. Even if a woman who was nothing but skin and bones married into the family, it would not matter because God would make her strong.

For example, if God causes a person to become a king, then even David, the shepherd, becomes king. When God made Joseph a governor, although he was a prisoner just a day before for the attempted rape of his master's wife, Joseph, who was locked in prison, became governor.

Abraham had the faith to believe. Before, however, he did not have the faith to believe in God and thus labored and strained to have a son himself. But now, he came to read the heart of God. He was 100 years old and his wife was so old that it had ceased to be with her after the manner of women. But regardless of that, Abraham had the faith that since it is God who will give him a son to fulfill His promise, ultimately God would accomplish His will.

Abraham was now free concerning the finding of a wife for Isaac. "I do not have to go to find a wife for my son." He thus sent his old servant from his household.

"Go and bring back the woman who will be my son, Isaac's wife."

Upon hearing Abraham's words that he should bring back the woman who would be his son's wife, the old servant was much burdened. Why? Abraham had the faith to believe in God, but the servant did not have that faith in his heart.

"I wish the master's son could come with me. . . ."

This way, he would then be free because now it would be a woman chosen by Isaac himself.

"What woman would see an old man like me and come along?"

He then asked Abraham, "If the woman does not want to follow me, why don't I take the master's son and show her the son to have her come with me?"

"Do not take my son there. Why should he go to the land God took us out of? God clearly promised that He will give me seed like the stars of the sky and the sands of the seashore. For this He has surely prepared Isaac's wife. Hence, go."

The old servant changed his heart upon listening to Abraham. "That's right. God has worked this way upon my master and He will have already prepared the master's daughter-in-law."

## Faith Is Confirming the Heart of God

Abraham became free from all things once knowing the heart of God. A great nation will be fulfilled through Isaac, and God planned to have the Messiah who would save mankind be born from among his descendants. Therefore, he believed that the will of God would be accomplished no matter what happened. Hence, Abraham felt completely free.

Many people are fooled into thinking that going to church, reading the Bible, and keeping the Word of God is believing in God. That is not faith. True faith is to know the heart of God and believe that God will accomplish everything. You must confirm this with the heart of God.

For example, suppose I went to a friend of mine to borrow money and for one reason or another he refuses. What I want to know is this friend's heart. "Does he have the intention of loaning me the money but cannot afford to? Or is he making excuses because he does not want to loan me the money?" I would try to feel my friend's heart. "Ah, this friend has no heart whatsoever to loan me the money." Then I do not need to speak to him about money again. On the other hand, if my friend said, "I apologize. I don't have the money right now, but I think there will be some money in my account tomorrow morning. Would it be okay for me to give you the money tomorrow morning?" I could confirm that my friend has the heart to loan me the money. Therefore, I will feel free.

Abraham believed his own thoughts before confirming the heart of God. However, he came to believe God through knowing the will and heart of God within the Word of God.

"God has made up His mind to give me a son. He has decided to give me many descendants through my son, Isaac. So He will do so!"

Because this assurance of faith entered Abraham's heart, there was no need for Abraham to labor in order to find a wife for Isaac because it was now God's work. God would do this. This is what spiritual life is.

## The Condition Is, "Is God Pleased with This?"

I have faced many difficulties as I have lived inside the Lord until now. When I began preaching the gospel, I tried to hold a retreat. We did not have a retreat site or money, so we came together every evening and held prayer meetings. The brothers would work hard all day long and come to the prayer services in the evenings. They would be so tired and would fall asleep while praying most of the time. One person would wake up, pray and fall asleep, then another person would pray and fall asleep. That was how the prayer meetings began. Since we had no means or methods, we prayed. After praying for about a week, it was amazing to see we were all gaining strength when we prayed, despite our fatigue.

After praying like this for about two weeks, nothing in the circumstances had changed, but we had the heart that God was pleased with us having a retreat. When we prayed a little longer, we had the heart, "God will allow us to have the retreat, if He is pleased!" Later, we had faith and prayers, such as, "God, thank you. We have no doubt that you will do this for us," flowed out freely from us. Now, our prayers did not end with worries or concerns, but with thankfulness. The time for the retreat was nearing and we still had no money, and there was nothing we could do. However, we felt so free and peaceful because we had faith towards God. Then we saw all of these things being accomplished.

After having had many such experiences, as I did the work of the gospel, I did not want to know, "Is this humanly possible or not?" but I rather wanted to know, "Is God pleased with this or not?"

When we first prayed, we prayed to God for our requests, but as we continued to pray, the heart of God became absorbed into us. As this continued for some time, we saw the heart of God and had faith, "Regardless of how this looks to man, it will be accomplished because it is the will of God!" Then we had true freedom. When our hearts became closer to God and we came to know God's heart, we had rest and God worked from that point on. I have continued to see how God often accomplishes what is humanly impossible.

## Once You Know the Heart of God

In receiving the forgiveness of sins, it is not that you have to find something in order to have the assurance of forgiveness of sin. Whether you are crying, have a burning sensation, are overwhelmed, or what not, such things are not important. You must search the heart of God because it is He who forgives sins, not you. We must open the Bible and seek the heart of God because we do not know the heart of God. Just as Abraham gained freedom concerning all things once he knew the heart of God, all things are taken care of for us concerning the problem of having our sins forgiven once we know what the heart of God is.

"Ah, God wants to wash my sins away. That is why He sent His son, Jesus. If He allowed His son to be crucified, why would He hesitate in washing my sins away? God had Jesus crucified so that my sins could be washed away. God would not have offered His son if my sins could not be washed away even through the death of Jesus on the cross. Then Jesus washed my sins away through being crucified! My sins are washed away!"

This is confirming with the Scriptures. Regardless of how it seems to you, if your sins are washed in the heart of God, they are washed. Read the heart of God in the Scriptures to confirm that your sins are washed away, and there you will gain the assurance of the forgiveness of sin. Saying, "I began to cry during prayer," "I felt a burning," or "My entire body was tingling," is not proof that you received the forgiveness of sin. Since it is God who forgives sin, you must gain the assurance of the forgiveness of sin not from yourself, but from God. It is difficult because people do not know this and try to gain assurance through their own emotions and feelings.

## Then God Will Accomplish!

For a long time Abraham had decided everything through his thoughts. But one day he saw, not his own heart, but the heart of God.

"God wants to give me a son."

He now clearly knew this.

"A great nation will be formed through this son. This can be done because this is the heart of God. In finding a daughter-in-law, God has prepared a wife that is best for Isaac. Therefore, it will not be a problem even if I do not go and only my old servant goes."

Abraham had this faith.

All the things I had to do also disappeared when I came to know the heart of God. I only need to believe because God has done everything to wash my sins away. I also saw that it was God who does the work of the gospel after salvation.

"This is how God works! Then God will accomplish everything!"

I had so much freedom and peace. Then, when I had this faith, I could see God working upon me.

In the Bible, there is a time when man is at work and a time when God is at work. It is always a problem when man is at work, but every time God works, all things become blessed. It is difficult when you try to do it yourself because you do not have the faith to believe in God. True faith is to know the heart of God, believe that He will work, and place your hope there.

# 36

# *The Holy Spirit Who Sanctifies Us*

*And the servant took ten camels, of the camels of his master, and departed; for all the goods of his master were in his hand: and he arose, and went to Mesopotamia, unto the city of Nahor. And he made his camels to kneel down without the city by a well of water at the time of the evening, even the time that women go out to draw water. And he said O LORD God of my master Abraham, I pray thee, send me good speed this day, and shew kindness unto my master Abraham. Behold, I stand here by the well of water; and the daughters of the men of the city come out to draw water: And let it come to pass, that the damsel to whom I shall say, Let down thy pitcher, I pray thee, that I may drink; and she shall say, Drink, and I will give thy camels drink also: let the same be she that thou hast appointed for thy servant Isaac; and thereby shall I know that thou hast shewed kindness unto my master.* (Genesis 24:10-14)

## For All the Goods of His Master Were in His Hand

I could feel myself becoming free as I read the Bible. I often felt, "Why didn't I know this before? I had not realized this. I was deceived because I did not know this!" whenever I discovered some truth in the Bible.

Genesis chapter 24 is about Abraham sending his old servant to bring back a wife for his son. When we read this closely, we can see that this is a parable of God sending the Holy Spirit to the church, the bride of Jesus Christ, in order to save it. This process is so precisely illustrated in much detail.

Verse 10 says, *And the servant took ten camels, of the camels of his master, and departed; for all the goods of his master were in his hand: and he arose, and went to Mesopotamia, unto the city of Nahor.* These words give me much hope and strength. Back then and even now, it is dangerous to carry gold or silver treasure around. However, here it says that the old servant was taking with him all the goods of his master in addition to the ten camels. The goods were probably all the good things of Abraham's house. Who brings all of their good things when going in search of a daughter-in-law? Moreover, the roads back then were not good, public safety was bad, and it was a time when there were lots of thieves. We cannot understand this very well, but there is hope for us because these Scriptures are telling us the process of God sending the Holy Spirit to seek the bride of Jesus Christ.

Abraham's old servant did not simply bring back a wife for Isaac, but decorated her with the best things of the master. A necklace, bracelet, earrings. . . . No matter what kind of a woman she was, even if she was a poor, pitiful woman, she was decorated beautifully and gloriously and taken back. In order to do this, the old servant brought the goods of his master with him.

## Unsparingly Gave Us All the Goods of Heaven

One day while I was wandering in sin, through faith, I came to realize that all of my sins were washed as white as snow and I received salvation. At the time, however, I only believed that the blood of Jesus washed all of my sins away. I still had many dirty and filthy aspects. As some time passed, I did not try to change but I discovered that my life was becoming more and more renewed and hopeful while living inside the guidance of the Holy Spirit.

This is how I feel in my heart each time I read Genesis chapter 24.

"That's right! Regardless of the bride's image, regardless of how sun-burnt she may be, she must have changed beautifully since piles of goods were brought upon ten camels. Likewise, after I receive salvation and become Christ's bride, God will generously give me everything of heaven to make me beautiful!"

Just as the goods of Abraham's house were brought unsparingly for one bride, God unsparingly gave us all the goods of heaven. The righteousness I did not have before was dwelling in me. And over time, I could see that the holiness I did not have before was dwelling in me; hope was dwelling in me; peace was dwelling in me; faith was dwelling in me; love was dwelling in me. . . . Such things were not coming from me, but were brought from heaven through the Holy Spirit as gifts from God. When I thought about this, I was so thankful.

Many years have passed since I received salvation and entered into Jesus Christ. When I look back, it was I who tried not to sin, to live as a good person and strained to be good, but all of that did not work. After being saved, however, God changed my heart without me even realizing it. As I have lived, I often felt so clearly that, "This is not my heart. This was not my heart, but this is the heart of Jesus Christ from God!"

God does not have me stand before Christ with nothing. Even though I had received salvation, I was truly a filthy, dirty, and deceitful human being. Just as Rebekah, who was to become Isaac's wife, was decorated with the treasures that filled the ten camels to stand before Isaac, God had me without blemish sanctified, beautified, cleansed, and glorified to stand before Jesus. When I think about such a loving God, I am so thankful.

I truly was a person who lived in the flesh, but God changed my life. One day, I saw that the heart of God was flowing in me. I was so filthy, dirty, lustful, and deceitful, yet a peace I did not have before flowed in me and joy flowed in me and faith flowed in me. I am so thankful to God when I see how I am changing into Jesus' likeness. I am more thankful that this is not through my effort or labor, but through God.

Not only am I this way but this is true with the people who come to my church, one by one. When they first came to church they were people who only lived tied to their flesh. But I saw that they changed as time passed by. "Ah, this is what God does!" It was truly amazing.

## According to the Old Servant's Prayer

Secondly, the old servant now had faith in his heart concerning the search for his master's daughter-in-law because he simply accepted Abraham's faith. He went to Mesopotamia and parked his camels near the well outside the city and prayed.

"God of my master, Abraham, allow me to meet the woman quickly and bestow grace unto my master, Abraham. There are women from the city who come to draw water. When I ask one, 'Give me a drink,' if she answers, 'I suppose that your camels are thirsty. I will draw water for them as well,' I will know that she is the one who will be my master's daughter-in-law."

Before he could finish his prayer, a beautiful woman

named Rebekah came to draw water. When the old servant said, "Give me a drink," Rebekah quickly let down the water-pot to have him drink and said, "I will also draw water for your camels so that they may drink." Camels drink lots of water and there were ten of them. The well is deep and it must be difficult to draw water but she was doing as the old servant had prayed. As the old servant quietly looked upon her actions, he thought, "God allowed a good path," and asked who she was and gave her the gifts. She was the daughter of his master's younger brother. The old servant quickly rejoiced, told Rebekah's family of this matter, and took her to Abraham's house.

When our church was preaching the gospel in China for the first time, we sent Missionary Kwang-bo Lee to China. At that time, he knew no one in China. A Korean Chinese named Nam-sook Hur came to Korea and heard the gospel while she was staying at my house for a few days. Missionary Lee wanted to meet her, who lived in Harbin. He had her address but wandered around because he had no idea how to go about finding her. He got on a city bus in Harbin and since he looked a little different from the Chinese there, a Korean-Chinese woman on the bus began to talk to him.

"Are you from Korea?"

"Yes."

"What brings you here?"

"I just came to Harbin."

"Do you know anyone here?"

"I do know one person."

"What is her name?"

"Her name is Nam-sook Hur."

"Oh, her? I know her well."

Millions of people live in Harbin but on that bus he met someone who knew Nam-sook Hur.

We run into many such instances when we do the work of God. This is because the work is God's and not ours.

## You Will Not Die Until You have Fulfilled the Duty God Gave You

It is difficult and tiring when we do things different from the will of God. But there is nothing difficult when doing things in accordance to the will of God. It is because God accomplishes everything, not you. Abraham had strained to have a child himself when he did not know this. If it were like the past, he would have said, "We can have good sons if we get a healthy daughter-in-law. Although she may appear healthy outwardly, you never know if she might be sick. We have to find a healthy daughter-in-law. . . ."

The daughter-in-law should be pretty and have class, but more than anything, she should be able to have children in order for Abraham to have a grandson. But how can you tell if a woman is good at child-bearing? Are there not women who are extremely healthy yet unable to have children? But upon knowing the will of God, Abraham did not have to worry about this. In the heart of the old servant as well, there was the assurance of faith in God, saying, "God will accomplish this, for this is God's will," upon hearing the words of Abraham.

I once called Missionary Gyung-hyun Nam, our missionary to the Philippines, on the phone and his son answered, telling me that his father was hospitalized. I asked him what for, and he answered that his father had Dengue Fever. This is a very scary febrile disease and unless treated in its early stages, the death rate is 95%. Missionary Nam had gone to the jungle to preach the gospel, but in just one day, his face and whole body began to turn dark. The church people of the Philippines rejoiced, saying, "Wow, the missionary will now become tanned just like us." They had no idea that this was from Dengue Fever and he had lost the window for treatment.

I called the National Medical Center where Missionary Nam was hospitalized. I asked for the emergency room and asked to speak with Missionary Nam. His wife answered and she began to weep and wail.

"Pastor! Now what do we do?"

She was telling me that since the treatment window had already passed, the doctors had given up already. I told her to stop crying. I told her that Missionary Nam will not die.

"Pastor Nam went to the Philippines not because the mission or I sent him there. God sent him there. There is a duty God has given to Pastor Nam for him to accomplish in the Philippines. He will not die without fulfilling it. He can rest after God accomplishes this through him and tells him to rest. He will not die because he caught Dengue Fever. He can go when God tells him to come. We can never simply die, even if we want to!"

That heart was in me, so I told her about this in detail. A few days later, Pastor Nam miraculously recovered his health.

It seems to us that some things are possible while some are not, but in the Bible we see that the will of God is accomplished.

## I Am What I Am

As I mentioned earlier, this story has, in detail, explained how God sent the Holy Spirit to save the bride of Jesus Christ, the groom, to take her to the wedding in heaven. The old servant did not simply take the bride, but decorated her beautifully. Likewise, it is showing us precisely how the Holy Spirit will make us beautiful when He takes us as Christ's bride.

I did not try to become good after becoming born again. How can I defeat sin and temptation? When the desires and ambitions of the flesh would arise, I did not have the power to suppress them. Like a crazy person I lived led by ambitions and desires. Jesus Christ, however, allowed me to overcome these desires and ambitions after He became the Lord of my heart. I saw this very often. This guidance was truly precious and beautiful.

Receiving forgiveness of sins is not through our efforts or good deeds. It must be through Jesus for there is nothing we can do. Living holy after receiving salvation is absolutely not through us as well. It is not through you doing good or ceasing to commit sins, but the Holy Spirit shears away our filth. Believe this. Just as the old servant brought all the goods on ten camels and decorated Rebekah, the Holy Spirit, from the storage in heaven, brings all the goods of heaven to us. He then decorates us to be holy, righteous, pure, blessed, and glorious. Even now, the Holy Spirit works within the born again saint. Therefore, it is not you fighting sin, and it is not you fighting temptation. Because the Holy Spirit fights instead of you, you can truly have grace, peace, and live blessedly. Just as Apostle

Paul said, "By the grace of God I am what I am," it is not through our goodness and effort.

When we look at Genesis chapter 24, verse by verse, we see that it was in this manner that God prepared everything for us. Are you filthy? Dirty? Deceitful? Change is not completed through you, but you are changed beautifully through the things God has prepared for you. That is what we call the process of becoming holy. It is us changing into the image of Jesus. God has prepared these amazing things for us because He loves us.

## For the Same Holy Spirit Is at Work

We are educating college students through an organization called the IYF (International Youth Fellowship). College students with grudges against their parents, bitterness towards society, and those who live only for their own flesh are extremely commonplace. However, when these students one day hear the gospel, they testify and realize that their sins were forgiven through the blood of Jesus Christ, their hearts become freed from sin, and their lives change. They are the same students, but their thinking changes. Before, they only cared about themselves, only following after the pleasures of the flesh, eating, and drinking. But now these students live for others, love the gospel and love the Lord. Did this happen because someone told them that they should have such hearts? They changed this way because the Holy Spirit led these students' hearts.

Amazing things happen when the gospel is preached. When we preach the gospel in Africa, America, or in India, people's thoughts change and their lives change. This is because it is the same Holy Spirit changing their hearts.

Our lives are not fulfilled through ourselves but through the providence and will of the almighty God. Our salvation is also not through our effort or labor, but completely through the blood of Jesus Christ. The only thing we can do is accept, by faith, the grace and love of God. Living a holy life through receiving salvation and not committing sin is also not done through us laboring and trying to do so, but through the Holy Spirit coming into our hearts and leading us.

## Let Us Hope and Believe in Him Who Will Sanctify

Loving folks, when we do not realize that God changes us to live precious lives, we try to carry those burdens ourselves. We labor to wash our sins away, and we try to become righteous, holy, and godly. It is because we do not know the world of faith that is believing in God. No matter how dirty or filthy we may be, when we come before God, He washes our sins away and makes us the children of God. In addition, he makes us holy, flawless, and spotless so that we may have no shame whatsoever to stand before Christ who is the groom. We must believe this promise of God, rely on God, and put hope in God. If we try to work ourselves without realizing this, it will become more difficult the more we try.

Just as Rebekah had lived in the countryside but became beautiful and glorious through meeting Abraham's old servant, I hope that you will surely remember that through meeting Jesus, we will live a blessed and beautiful life.

# 37

# *The Cursed Path of Esau and the Blessed Path of Jacob*

*And it came to pass, that when Isaac was old, and his eyes were dim, so that he could not see, he called Esau his eldest son, and said unto him, My son: and he said unto him, Behold, here am I. And he said, Behold now, I am old, I know not the day of my death: Now therefore take, I pray thee, thy weapons, thy quiver and thy bow, and go out to the field, and take me some venison; And make me savoury meat, such as I love, and bring it to me, that I may eat; that my soul may bless thee before I die.* (Genesis 27:1-4)

## The Stories of the Bible That Reveal the Spiritual World

I become very thankful before God when I read Genesis. The stories of Genesis seem like just ordinary stories. However, only a few stories have been selected to be recorded out of the many events that happened on earth at the time Genesis was being recorded. Abraham's life, Jacob's life, Joseph's life. . . .

No matter how thick the book, it would not be enough to record all of their lives. God did not simply record stories in the Bible, but did so to have us realize the spiritual meaning inside the stories.

When I first began reading the Bible, I simply read through it. But as I read it more and more, the Holy Spirit showed me the worlds of the human heart and the heart of God. I came to know, "Ah, that's what these words mean!" As the words began to enter my heart, I was able to precisely see my image through the Bible.

"That's how this person was, and his heart is like mine. Ah, this story is about me."

Then I could understand why Christians of the past called the Bible the mirror of the heart. At first I read the Bible as a story; as an incident. But as I discovered the heart of God and my image, which were hidden there, I discovered, "That's why I was in darkness; that's why I was distant from God; and that's why there was a problem between me and God!" and I became freed from those things. It was so amazing how my image was shown in the Bible.

The story of Genesis chapter 27, if simply read, appears to be just an ordinary story. Isaac had two sons: Esau and Jacob. To give away the blessings, Isaac called Esau and said, "Take me some venison; and make me savoury meat, such as I love, and bring it to me, that I may eat; that my soul may bless thee before I die." Upon hearing this, Esau took his quiver and his bow, hunted, made a dish, and brought it before his father.

"Father, as you have commanded I have hunted and made a dish for you. Eat, and bless me freely."

The father was stunned.

"What! There was one who had just brought something from hunting to me. Who was he?"

It was found that Jacob had taken the blessing. How did Jacob receive the blessing? Because Jacob was unqualified to be blessed, his mother made him savoury meat from a kid of the goats, camouflaged Jacob with fur to feel like Esau, and had him blessed through sending him forth using Esau's name.

From Esau's point of view, it seems that he had been wronged. All he did was what his father told him: he hunted, made savoury meat, and brought it to his father. But ultimately, the father did not bless Esau but cursed him.

"Behold, thy dwelling place shall be the fatness of the earth, and of the dew of heaven from above, and by thy sword thou shalt live, and shalt serve thy brother. . . ."

These words are not merely words. God put His heart into these words. What heart did He put in?

## We Who Feel Different from the Word of God

God often speaks to us through the Bible, and Jeremiah chapter 17 tells us, *The heart is deceitful above all things, and desperately wicked.* I read much of the Bible. After I read these words a few times, I passed them by, thinking, "That's right. Man's heart is evil. It is wicked." But I have never felt the heart of God that called my heart deceitful above all things and desperately wicked. I thought, in my own way, "I am evil. I am dirty. I'm deceitful. I'm filthy." That was why, even though I read, memorized, and spoke the Word, my heart was so different from the heart of God.

For example, upon hearing, "I've eaten," Koreans will think of rice, dwenjang-soup, and kimchi. Germans may think of eating bread and sausage with wine. Although both are referring to the same word, "eating," the feelings are completely different. God sees the heart of man and says that it is dirty, evil, and rotten beyond comparison with anything. However, we humans take it as, "Yeah, we humans are all evil. Who isn't evil?" The wickedness that man calls wicked and what God calls wicked may be said using the same words, but they hold completely different meanings.

I, too, thought that I was evil. But I could not feel the evilness in me that God felt. Therefore, I thought, "I am evil. But I'll be okay if I am good, sincere, and live my spiritual life well from now on." Then one day, I received the grace of God. I feel that God allowed me to borrow His eyes to see myself, not how I saw myself until then. When I saw myself that day, I was so pitiful, dirty, and filthy. It was beyond comparison with how I had felt about myself up till then. Before, I thought, "So what if I lie a little? Is there anyone who doesn't lie?" and knew that I was a bit wicked but thought of myself as a good person. That day, however, God allowed me to borrow His eyes, and when He had me see the wickedness He saw and not the wickedness I saw with my own eyes, then I could finally realize how evil I was.

"Man is indeed truly dirty! Man deserves to be cursed and destroyed!"

When I simply felt that I was evil, I thought if I do good, keep the law, and live spiritual life, I would be able to go to heaven. But when I saw myself through the eyes of God, I was a person who, regardless of what I did, was perfectly fit to go to hell.

## In the Eyes of God

People read the Bible. They also have service and pray. But although they are reading the same Scriptures, what they feel and what God speaks of, though they may be using the same words, mean completely different things. Since the world is so dirty and evil, you cannot feel your evilness even though you are evil. You see yourself with the standard of the person next to you because you cannot see yourself through the standard of God.

"That man, even though he believes in Jesus and is an elder, is full of baloney. I'm not like him."

That is why people believe themselves to be good. Although you are dirty, you believe that you are not very dirty because you have some good parts. Now, this is where the problem arises. What problem? In the standard of God, we humans are so evil that we cannot become good through human effort. Therefore, God gave up on man becoming good. However, man does not think this way. Man thinks, "Yes, I did sin, I did do some evil. But there is some good in me. If I live an honest and truthful life, I will become holy. I can go to heaven."

In the eyes of God, there is no good in man no matter how much man does good. Psalms chapter 14 says, *The LORD looked down from heaven upon the children of men, to see if there were any that did understand, and seek God. They are all gone aside, they are all together become filthy: there is none that doeth good, no, not one.* Man is extremely evil in the eyes of God. But since we live amidst the evilness, we think of ourselves to be good, if we are just a little better than others. We do not know that we are evil even though we are. Thus, we believe that we can become good if we strive to be good and diligent. People all have this kind of heart. Therefore, they try to do well.

That is why God gave the law to man. God did not give you the law for you to keep it and do good and go to heaven. If you try to keep the law, you come to realize how evil and dirty you are. God gave you the law for you to realize, "I can only be cursed and destroyed!" and have you give up on you trying to do good, and have you accept the righteousness of Jesus Christ. Nevertheless, most people do not know this and think that they can go to heaven if they keep the law well.

## Bless Me, O My Father!

God wanted to teach us these facts. Today, through the story of "Jacob and Esau," He wants to teach us about this.

Esau listened to what his father said. He said, "Take your quiver and bow, hunt, and make me the savoury meat such as I love. I will eat and bless thee." Esau listened to his father and went out exactly as he said. He was sweating much as he ran around trying to catch an animal. Catching an animal is no easy task, and bringing home that animal he has caught is also no easy task. Try carrying from deep in the mountains a dead deer, boar, or roe that weighs 200 lbs. How tiring would that be?

Esau was drenched in sweat as he caught the animal and cooked it. He made a dish and brought it before his father. Esau said, "Now God made a promise to my grandfather, Abraham, and made a promise to my father. Now I will be receiving that blessing. The blessing that God promised is mine!" and with high expectations, he went before his father.

"Father, I have hunted and made savoury meat as you have said. Eat, and let your soul bless me."

Then his father became surprised.

"Who are you?"

"What do you mean, 'Who are you?' Father, you told me that you would bless me if I hunted an animal and made savoury meat. I'm Esau."

The father trembled in shock and spoke.

"Then who was the one who brought me venison just a while ago? Who was the one I just blessed upon eating before you came here? He will surely be blessed."

"What? I brought the savoury meat that I hunted and cooked! What do you mean someone was here?"

"No, Esau was here before you came. I freely ate his savoury meat and blessed him with all my soul."

"It was Jacob! Only Jacob would do such a thing!" Esau spoke to his father.

"Father, do you have even one blessing to give? Father, bless me as well. I did what you said. Bless me also, O my father!" Esau cried and besought his father, but his father refused him.

"Behold, I have made him thy lord, and all his brethren have I given to him for servants; and with corn and wine have I sustained him: and what shall I do now unto thee, my son?"

Esau lifted his voice, cried, and clung to his father.

"Hast thou but one blessing, my father? Bless me, even me also, O my father!"

The father then said this to Esau, "Behold, thy dwelling shall be the fatness of the earth, and of the dew of heaven from above; and by thy sword thou shalt live, and thou shalt serve thy brother, and it shall come to pass when thou shalt have the dominion, that thou shalt break his yoke from off thy neck."

Esau thought surely that he would be blessed if he hunted and brought the savoury meat as the father had promised but he was cursed.

## For There Are Many Who Walk the Path of Esau

Why did God write these words in the Bible? It means that there are many people today who live their spiritual life like

Esau. It means that there are so many people who, in their spiritual life, believe that they will be blessed if they keep the law according to God's words, go to church on Sundays, give tithes, and come before God. God wrote this story in the Bible because He wanted to teach us, "You will be cursed if you do that. You will be destroyed if you live like that. You cannot be blessed if you continue that way."

Most people, when they go to church, think, "That's right. I sinned as I went to church, but I will be blessed by God if I live according to the Word of God and live diligently. God will bless me." This thought comes from not knowing the heart of God that, *The heart is deceitful above all things and desperately wicked.*

God knew that man was truly filthy and dirty. God knew that in the heart of man, hatred burns in the deep corners of the heart of man, lies take their place, lust comes from there, and hatred comes pouring out. How could such a man do good and obtain righteousness? The good that comes from man may appear good in the eyes of man, but since the nature of the heart of man is dirty and filthy, good cannot come forth. How can good be done when the nature itself is evil and dirty? It is impossible. That is what God wanted to show us.

Therefore, we see in the Bible that all those who tried to be blessed by God through being loyal to the Word of God were all cursed. All those who try to keep the commandments and be blessed through being loyal all become cursed. The most representative story of this is the story of Genesis chapter 27.

## Walk the Path of Jacob

Then what must we do to be blessed? We must walk the path of Jacob. Jacob knew that he was a dirty human who had no chance whatsoever at being blessed. Since he knew that he could not be blessed, he hid himself, went forth in the name of his brother Esau, and was blessed. In other words, we are blessed through the power of Jesus.

"God, I cannot be good no matter how much I try. My heart is evil by nature, and what good can ever come from this evil heart of mine?"

Therefore, you must cover yourself. The good that you have done, your honesty, the righteousness you have, the help you gave to others, you have to throw all these things into the trash and hear what Jesus Christ has done. You must receive the power of Jesus, become one with Him, and come before God. That is what the Bible is talking about.

I am not righteous, but I am righteous if I have the righteousness of Jesus. I am not holy, but I am if I have the holiness of Jesus. To do this, God sent Jesus to this earth. Jesus lived in the land of Judea for 33 years without having sinned once. He lived holy and righteously. Then He ascended into heaven. God gave to us the holy life Jesus lived for the 33 years He was alive. Jesus took away the lifelong sinfulness of us. Jesus took our sins and became a sinner in our stead and gave His holy life to us. We became righteous through the righteousness of Jesus and were made to be able to come before God.

Jesus lived in this world without sinning and was crucified. Why was that so? It was because Jesus bore our sins. The moment our sins were moved on to Jesus, the righteousness and holiness of Jesus moved over on to us. Whether we know it or not, our sins have moved on to Jesus and Jesus became the sinner, while the righteousness and holiness of Jesus came upon us to make us righteous.

When we come before God, we do not come forth through keeping the law and doing good deeds. Although you have done good deeds, you must throw away your heart completely because it is, by nature, evil and dirty. You must come forth through the righteousness and holiness of Jesus He has given you. Genesis chapter 27 is telling us that at that instant we can be blessed.

Jacob completely erased himself. He only brought the dish Rebekah prepared and came in the name of his brother, Esau, to be blessed. Esau brought forth what he did well, how he hunted and cooked the meat according to his father's words, and was cursed. Today, the Bible is clearly teaching us about this. You are cursed if you come forth with the good things you have done well. But if you deny yourself and bring forth the righteousness and holiness of Jesus, you are blessed by God. Genesis chapter 27 is clearly expounding this to us.

# 38

## *I Am Esau, Thy Firstborn!*

*And Rebekah heard when Isaac spake to Esau his son. And Esau went to the field to hunt for venison, and to bring it. And Rebekah spake unto Jacob her son, saying, Behold, I heard thy father speak unto Esau thy brother, saying, Bring me venison, and make me savoury meat, that I may eat, and bless thee before the LORD before my death. Now therefore, my son, obey my voice according to that which I command thee. Go now to the flock, and fetch me from thence two good kids of the goats; and I will make them savoury meat for thy father, such as he loveth: And thou shalt bring it to thy father, that he may eat, and that he may bless thee before his death.* (Genesis 27:5-10)

## Biblical Repentance

Spiritual life is composed of "repentance" and "faith." Repentance is turning from our current path because it is crooked and wrong. Then it is possible to have faith to believe in God. The greatest reason spiritual life does not succeed is because people do not know precisely what repentance is and, therefore, is not properly achieved. Spiritual life is so easy if you discover yourself and repent, no matter who you are.

I learned about repentance as I attended church as a young child. The pastor taught us that saying, "I stole. I lied. I hated others," and confessing our wrongdoings before God was repentance. I continued doing such repentance to a certain extent, but when I would repent in this manner, I would sin again, repent again, and then sin again. My life was just a repetitious cycle of sinning and repenting and sinning and repenting. My life of sin, however, would not end even though I had repented. That was the constant existence of my spiritual life.

To have a greater faith than others, although I felt sleepy, I would wake up early in the morning, go to early-morning prayer services and confess my sins. My spiritual life was going to church and emptying my heart whenever it would be filled with sin. However, people labeled me a person with a good spiritual life. I was filthy with many evil things inside me, but I felt good that others were saying that my faith was good.

As I read the Bible from then on, I came to know that Biblical repentance was completely different from what I had learned from my church pastor in my childhood. God did not want me to confess the symptoms, saying, "I stole something. I committed adultery. I lied. I hated." The Bible was talking about our dirty nature, about how we could only steal, could only lie, and could only be lustful.

After David committed adultery with Uriah's wife, what did he write in Psalms when he was confessing his sin? He did not say, "God, desires arose in me when I saw her, so I committed adultery," confessing the actual adultery. Rather, he confessed, *I was shapen in iniquity; and in sin did my mother conceive me.* (Psalms 51:5) We can see the image of David confessing before God, that he was by nature, a cluster of sin.

## If You Catch the Disease of Sin

If one catches leprosy, there are symptoms such as one's eye brows falling off, fingers getting cut off, and the nerves becoming paralyzed. When these things happen, one should not try to keep his eye brows or fingers from falling off. It is the bacteria that is affecting the body. One should not try to fix the paralysis in the nerves, but treat the source of leprosy, which is the leprosy bacteria.

Just as there are many symptoms when one has leprosy, there are a variety of symptoms when one catches the disease of sin. Symptoms from typhoid or malaria are quite obvious, like high fever, but when one catches the disease of sin, hatred arises, distrust arises, lust arises. . . . Many kinds of sin arise. The fact that you have committed adultery, committed thievery, or committed murder is merely the fruit or result of the sin in you. Such things are not the root of sin itself. Since adultery, murder, and theft come from the evil characteristics in you, it is not that you should confess these symptoms before God. But as you see these symptoms, you must say, "This is how dirty and evil my insides are!" and repent, distrusting yourself who had the dirty heart. This is true repentance.

If you turn from yourself, saying, "I committed theft," the heart to steal arises in you again. You make confessions, saying, "I committed adultery," but a lustful heart arises in you, and when you feel regret, saying, "I lied," another deceitful heart arises in you. Because everything that arises in you is evil and deceitful by nature, you must distrust all things that arise in your heart. It is saying, "I cannot do good because I am evil and deceitful! I cannot do righteous deeds!"

When I attended church as a child, I appeared to be good outwardly because I tried to live better than other children. Thus, I thought I was good, and that, to a certain extent, if I tried hard, I could go to heaven. However, one day, I saw my image reflected through the eyes of God. Before this moment,

I had the heart, "Who does not sin? Still, I did not commit any great sins." Nevertheless, when I saw myself that day, I realized what a dirty, filthy, and evil person I was. I came to know that I could only be cursed. I was full of hatred, lust, and wickedness, and therefore, I came to know that all the good I did was fake; they were hypocritical good deeds only to cover my evilness. I had no way and no hope in front of God.

## The Two Paths to Come Before God

Like we talked about in the last sermon, Genesis chapter 27 illustrates the images of two individuals who went before God to be blessed. Esau, in accordance to the words of his father, hunted an animal himself and bore the heavy animal on his shoulders, climbing over mountains as he sweated much to reach his house. Then he skinned the animal, made savory meat, and served it to his father. He should have surely been blessed, but Esau was cursed.

What did Jacob do? Since he was too evil and dirty, he had no confidence that he would be blessed by his father. Thus, he said to his mother, Rebekah, "Mother, my brother Esau is a hairy man, and I am a smooth man. My father peradventure will feel me, and I shall seem to him as a deceiver; and I shall bring a curse upon me, and not a blessing." Rebekah answered, "Upon me be thy curse, my son: only obey my voice and go fetch me them." Jacob realized that it was impossible for him to labor and to try on his own to come before his father to be blessed. Therefore, he did not rely on himself, but with faith to trust in what his mother, Rebekah, prepared, he went before his father and was blessed.

Esau is a foreshadow of people who try to be blessed through doing good deeds and doing well themselves. Jacob, on the contrary, is the image of a person who cannot be blessed, but cursed, because he is filthy and dirty. There are two ways to come before God. One is to rely on your effort, labor, and works. On the surface, this appears to be belief in God, but this is not belief in God. It is belief in one's self. The other way is to rely only on God because there is no good in you. Only this is the true faith to believe in God.

## I Am Esau

When Rebekah told Jacob to only obey her words in Genesis chapter 27, Jacob answered, "My brother Esau is a hairy man, and I am a smooth man. My father peradventure will feel me, and I shall bring a curse upon me, and not a blessing." Then Rebekah said, "Upon me be thy curse, my son." While reading this verse once, I was able to realize its meaning. The only one who can say, "Upon me be thy curse," is the Son of God, Jesus Christ. No one can take the place of our sins or receive the curse in our place.

"Rebekah represents Jesus Christ who bore our sins and was punished in our place!"

Then I read the verses that followed. Esau went before the father with the fruits of his labor and sweat. Jacob completely went forward exactly with what his mother, Rebekah, prepared. He followed his mother's will and went forward with the dish she cooked. In addition, since Jacob was a smooth person, his mother decorated Jacob with goat skin so that he would lack nothing in standing before his father. Jacob trusted his mother and went forward wearing what his mother prepared for him.

His father, Isaac, asked Jacob, "Who are you?"

"I am your firstborn Esau," Jacob replied.

Jacob did not call himself Jacob, but Esau. He completely cast himself away. His own image, his own goodness. . . . Jacob did not say, "Father, remember the good deed I did that one time? I obeyed you. Remember that and bless me." He threw himself away and only took what his mother prepared for him and went before his father.

"I am your firstborn Esau."

This verse is so amazing. It is because it depicts the love and grace Jesus bestowed on to us. Jesus not only took care of our sins when He was crucified, but also gave to us the goodness, holiness, and the righteousness of the 33 years of His life. Lastly, He gave us His own name. He allowed us to use His name freely. Therefore, when we pray, we do not pray in our name, but in the name of Jesus. When you withdraw money from the bank you can get it only with the name of the account holder. Likewise, we turn in the form in the name of Jesus when we seek from God.

Now we come before God in the name of Jesus.

"Who are you?"

"I am Jesus."

Is this right? It is right! It is all because Jesus gave us His name for us to use. We not only pray in the name of Jesus, but we have now died and have become a part of Jesus. On the surface we are ourselves, but inside we are Jesus.

"Who are you?"

"I am Jesus."

"Ah, is that so?"

God does not want you to become a little better than the dirty, filthy person you are and then come forth to Him. Because you are a dirty sinner, He throws you away and accepts only Christ. What happens when Jacob goes before his father in his own name?

"Yes, father, I am Jacob."

"Why did you come? I asked for Esau. Leave immediately!"

He would have been kicked out. But Jacob went out in the name of Esau. His father then felt him.

"Let me feel you to see if you are Esau."

The amazing thing about this is that since his mother, Rebekah, knows the father so well, she made the food to fit the father's taste, and she also knew that his father would feel Jacob. Thus, she put Esau's clothes on Jacob and decorated him with goat skins like Esau.

Just as Rebekah did this to Esau, Jesus does this to us and speaks to us.

"Do not do good for yourself and bring it forth to God. These may look good in your eyes but in the eyes of God, they are like filthy rags, deceitful above all things, and desperately wicked. Throw everything of yourself away, and do not live your life; you shall live My life. No matter what you do from now on, do it in My name."

"Yes, I understand. Now I am dead, and Jesus, who is not me, lives in me. Now I am Jesus."

We have blemishes and are dirty, but since Jesus is perfect, we come before God believing and relying on the fact that Jesus has given us His righteousness and His name. Right then,

God joyfully accepts you. This is what Genesis chapter 27 is telling us.

## From the Life of Trusting Yourself to the Life of Trusting Jesus

People think that things will go well if they simply try hard and keep the law in their spiritual lives. God wanted to teach us the fact that this will not cause our spiritual lives to succeed.

Esau hunted and made a dish according to the father's words but was cursed. However, Jacob did not do anything at all. He went forth to his father with all the things his mother prepared. Jacob's mother prepared and completed everything so that he would lack nothing in coming before his father to be blessed. She even promised that she would receive the curse that would come upon Jacob. This is what Jesus did to us. Jesus received the curse we should have received, and prepared all things for us to be glorified and blessed. We need only to come before God in the name of Jesus Christ.

I did not know this for a long time, and I tried to go before God through my good deeds. Therefore I felt free to come before God when I had tithed and had done good deeds. In contrast, I felt ashamed to come before God when I had fought, lied, or done something bad. In reality, I often committed wickedness in my life and I always went before God with a shameful heart, begging for forgiveness with my tears. I did not know that was wrong, but later found out that this was something that was in contempt with God. I was not accepting what Jesus prepared for me, but was trying to do good myself to come before God. I later on realized that God was not pleased by this.

Now, I do not come before God through myself. Because my nature is evil and false, I completely distrusted myself as a whole and threw away everything I had done. Then the good committed not by me, but Jesus, became my goodness; my righteousness. Since everything Jesus did became mine, I felt so free coming before God. Now I do not trust myself. I trust Jesus. I am a filthy, dirty human being, but I believe in Jesus who cleansed me and justified me through the blood of the cross so that I may lack nothing to stand before God.

As my life changed in this manner, from a life of trusting myself to a life of trusting Jesus, the Holy Spirit began to work amazingly inside of me. Before, I could not do any good even when I tried. But my life changed as the Holy Spirit began to take charge of my life. My flesh was still dirty, and evil things constantly sprang up. However, when Jesus was not inside me, such things dragged me around. But since Jesus conquers them, I am no longer dragged by them. I defeat sin and I can see that Jesus chisels me into the life with which God is pleased.

## Like Riding an Airplane on a Snowy Day

Believing in God is not believing in yourself. It is throwing yourself away because you are filthy and dirty, and then believing in Jesus. This is like not traveling in a car on a snowy day because the roads are too slippery, but going on the trip by plane. When you are riding in an airplane, what does it matter that it is snowing and that the roads are slippery? If we likewise rely on Jesus to come before God, so what if you are dirty and so what if you are deceitful? I lack much and have weaknesses even now, but I come before God boldly because I come through the righteousness, not of myself, but of Jesus.

Jacob had no conditions by which he could be blessed by his father. His mother prepared all things for him to be blessed, and Jacob was blessed by believing in them. Jesus has, in the same manner, prepared all things for us to stand before God without lacking anything. Therefore, we stand before God relying on this. I have no doubt that then God accepts us joyfully and bestows His grace onto us.

Loving folks, many people try to exalt their own righteousness in front of God. Many try to come before God with their own goodness and holiness. This is completely useless. If you become freed from yourself and become strengthened by Jesus, your image does not matter at all. Esau, who tried to be blessed through his sincere efforts, was cursed, and Jacob, who received his mother's grace, was blessed. If you come before God with your actions, you are cursed. When we come before God with the faith to believe in Jesus who died on the cross for us, I believe that grace and blessing will then overflow in us.

# 39

## *When Jacob Saw*

*And Jacob went out from Beersheba, and went toward Haran. And he lighted upon a certain place, and tarried there all night, because the sun was set; and he took of the stones of that place, and put them for his pillows, and lay down in that place to sleep. And he dreamed, and behold a ladder set up on the earth, and the top of it reached to heaven: and behold the angels of God ascending and descending on it. And, behold, the LORD stood above it, and said, I am the LORD God of Abraham thy father, and the God of Isaac: the land whereon thou liest, to thee will I give it, and to thy seed; And thy seed shall be as the dust of the earth, and thou shalt spread abroad to the west, and to the east, and to the north, and to the south: and in thee and in thy seed shall all the families of the earth be blessed.* (Genesis 28:10-14)

## What Do You See?

People's hearts are all different, but first of all, it is the desires of the flesh that lead the heart. You want to eat when you are hungry; you want to drink when you are thirsty; you want to be warm when you are cold. . . . There are desires such as these that are of the flesh. Then, sequentially, Satan puts other hearts inside of us. For example, just as Satan planted into the heart of Judas Iscariot the thought to sell Jesus, Satan also gives you the heart to follow your desires or the pleasures of the flesh. Then, when the occasion arises, your thoughts emerge dependent upon what you see. You think to eat bread when you see some, and you think, "I would like to eat that," when a certain dish comes into sight. I've heard that this is why television advertising is much more effective than radio advertising in drawing people's hearts. There are differences depending upon the individual, but for the most part, these kinds of things lead the hearts of people. Therefore, there are those who are able to control their own hearts in the midst of this, but there are those who simply leave themselves to flow according to the desires of their heart.

"What do you see?" is very important in spiritual life. In the Scriptures we are discussing today, the phrase, "Jacob saw," is constantly repeated. Towards the beginning of these Scriptures, a verse says, "Esau saw. . . ."

*When Esau saw that Isaac had blessed Jacob, and sent him away to Padan-aram, to take him a wife from thence; and that as he blessed him he gave him a charge, saying, Thou shalt not take a wife of the daughters of Canaan;* (Genesis 28:6)

Then it says in verse 8,

*And Esau seeing that the daughters of Canaan pleased not Isaac his father.*

What Esau saw was the humanistic circumstance that, "I took a woman of Canaan as a wife, and my father was not pleased." However, Jacob looked to God. Jacob saw a ladder reaching to heaven and there were angels ascending and descending upon it. Then God gave him a promise.

"Jacob, I am the God of Abraham, the God of Isaac, and your God. I will give the land you are laying on to you and your seed."

## Depending on Where Your Heart Flows

Regardless of how much you want to live spiritual life well, you can only live a fleshly life if your heart constantly flows toward the flesh. On the contrary, you can only live a spiritual life if your heart flows toward God.

Let me speak to you about Abraham. God one day promised Abraham, "Get thee out of thy country, and from thy kindred, and from thy father's house, unto a land that I will shew thee. And I will make of thee a great nation." Upon hearing this, Abraham had the heart, "God will make me into a great nation. He will give me many children like the stars in the sky and the sands of the sea." But as time passed, he saw the circumstances and saw that he was in no condition to have a child. He was too old and it had ceased to be with Sarah after the manner of women. God then reappeared to Abraham when he was 99 years old.

"As for Sarai thy wife, thou shalt not call her name Sarai, but Sarah shall her name be. I will bless her and she shall bear thee a son."

Right then what did Abraham say?

"Shall a child be born unto him that is an hundred years old? Sarah is ninety. . . ."

He was filled with human thoughts rather than the Word of God, and it seemed in the humanly view that he could not have a child. "Sarah could not have a child even in her younger years. How can she have a child at such an old age?" Abraham's heart simply flowed in a humanly way.

As I live spiritual life, sometimes my heart is close to God's, I long for God, and I pray deeply to God. When I am this way and problems arise, because I am close with God, in my heart I feel, "Is this my problem? It is God's problem, so He will take care of it blessedly." Then I am at peace and filled with joy. It is not because there are no problems; there still are, but I can live with thankfulness and joy. On the contrary, I become worried and concerned when confronted with problems when my heart is far from God's.

God dwelling and working in me is always the same. Whether I have faith or not, because God loves me, He works the same in me. However, when I am far from God and then face problems, it feels as though God will not take care of them and I become worried and concerned. I can feel such things very clearly as I minister.

When I argue with my wife, I strongly feel, "She is such a big problem!" in my heart when my heart is far from God. On the contrary, when I am close to God and the word is living inside me, in my heart I feel, "There can be some differences in opinion when we are trying to put forth our good thoughts. How can we think the same? What my wife is saying has merit too. God is leading both my wife and me." In this manner, such scenarios are the same concerning every problem, whether it is family or church problems.

## Satan Is Always at Work

When we search the Bible closely, God always promised us, and Satan always worked after the promise. God told Adam and Eve that they would surely die if they ate from the fruit of the knowledge of good and evil. But the serpent said, "No. You will not surely die. If you eat it, your eyes will be opened and you'll become like God." These two words are complete opposites. If we continue to hear only the Word of God, we think,

"If we eat this we will die!" But if we hear the voice of the serpent, in our hearts, we become people who think, "Die? Why would I die?"

This was also true at the time of Noah's flood. God said that He would judge the world with water, but Satan put another thought into the people's hearts.

"Why would the God of love destroy us? Since we are living sinfully these days, He is only telling us to stop sinning. Now all we have to do is return to God and live as good people."

God judges when He says that He will judge. However, Satan puts a thought into people and the people follow that thought. Noah, who received the Word of God, had the judgment come upon his heart, but the judgment did not come upon the other people's hearts. Thus, they had no need to make an ark although Noah was making one, and they felt no need to enter the ark when Noah entered in.

Not only is God in the world, but Satan is at work as well, and these things will only continue. One day, God anointed David and said that He would make him the king of Israel. How thankful do you think David was when he heard that? Satan afterwards gave him circumstances that were completely opposite. King Saul tried to kill David and he could no longer stay in the country. He had to run away to the Philistines. There is no time period for his return to Israel; his wife married another man. . . . In this way the circumstances were all full of despair and it seemed unlikely that David would become king.

God gives promises so that you can believe, and Satan works through circumstances to make it seem that that promise would not be achieved. Therefore, ultimately all things are decided by where we place our hearts, to which words we incline our ears, and to what we look towards.

## What Esau Saw and What Jacob Saw

Esau saw the humanistic aspects. "Father is not pleased of me taking a Canaan woman to wife." Therefore, to please his father, he took another woman to wife. Jacob, Esau's twin, was different. Jacob saw God. ". . . behold a ladder set up on the earth, and on it the angels of God were ascending and descending." The Bible also says, "and behold. . . ." When he first saw things, all he saw was that. But when he beheld again, God was there.

*I am the Lord God of Abraham thy father, and the God of Isaac: the land whereon thou liest, to thee will I give it, and to thy seed:* (Genesis 28:13)

He received the promise:

*I am with thee, and will keep thee in all places whither thou goest, and will bring thee again into this land;* (Genesis 28:15)

Jacob could act boldly upon receiving the promise: "God is with me! God is with me no matter where I go!"

## Joseph Dreamt

The Bible does not only contain stories of Jacob. God also, one day, showed a dream to Joseph. Joseph was binding sheaves and Joseph's sheaf stood up while his brothers' sheaves all bowed down to his. God had shown Joseph the promise that he would become a governor. God then had Joseph dream a second dream and it was one where the sun, moon, and eleven stars were bowing down to him. "God wants to make me into a governor!" Joseph believed the promise God showed him. But afterwards, what kind of things did Satan do to Joseph? Did everything go well according to the dream? Not at all. One day, Joseph was sold away as a slave.

"What? I am supposed to become the governor, but I am becoming a slave."

Satan continually put thoughts into Joseph's heart.

"What do you mean you are going to become a governor? Not you. You are a slave."

Joseph was working as a servant in the house of Potiphar, but as if this were not bad enough, one day, he refuses the temptations of Potiphar's wife and is taken as a rapist, and thrown into prison.

"God, is this the way to become the governor? I truly lived honestly and clean, but I am in prison. How could this be?"

When we turn just a single page from this scene, it talks about Joseph becoming the governor, doesn't it? However, since Joseph cannot see the next page, he could only see the scene of himself being in prison. Satan continually stirred up thoughts in Joseph's heart.

"How can you become a governor? That is impossible. Your life is continually turning for the worse. Why didn't God protect you when you were being sold as a slave? God does not love you. You served as a slave, and then you were ensnared by Potiphar's wife and ended up in prison. If you lived so truthfully, why would God keep you in prison? God has abandoned you. Now give up on everything, drink, eat, and live however you want and end your life!"

## You Hear the Voice of God, but the Voice of Satan as Well

It is not that many people do not hear the voice of God. They do hear the voice of God, but they also listen to the voice of Satan at the same time. Satan continually shows us the circumstances that make it seem like it will not work, and tells us that things will not work. Since we listen to Satan's voice, it even appears to our eyes that it will not work.

I once met a lady who had a morbid suspicion of her husband's fidelity. She claimed that her husband slept with another woman. I asked her, "How did you find this out?"

"Pastor, when I'm asleep, I'm no different than a dead body."

"Then how did you find this out?"

This lady, one day, opened her eyes in the morning and suddenly had the heart that her husband spent the night with a single woman who lived in an apartment building across the street, although she had not actually seen anything and it didn't happen.

I explained this to her in detail.

"There is no proof and you have no basis for what you are saying. Where do you think that heart came from? Satan put that heart in you to destroy your family."

Too many people today are led by thoughts that Satan put into them. We, too, are this way. Although something is not true, Satan leads our hearts to make it feel as if it were true. Thus, when we do not have faith, we read the Bible and listen to the words of God, but so many people live having believed the voices Satan put into them. They cannot commit to one side or the other, but they simply wander about before they end their lives.

People who believe God should not listen to the voices of their own heart, but to the Word of God. Joseph closed his eyes to see the humanly things and did not listen to his human thoughts. No matter the circumstances; no matter the sounds that arose in him; he looked up to the promise of God.

## If You Now Remain in the Promise of God like Jacob

Jacob looked to God, but Esau heard humanistic sounds and placed his heart there. This is what distinguishes people with faith from people without faith in spiritual life.

If you only think about your spirit; only about sin; you would close your ears to everything else and would open the Bible to heed the Word of God. The Bible tells us that Jesus bore all of our sins, was crucified, and died on the cross. The Bible clearly records that our sins have been washed as white as snow and that God will no longer condemn us of our sins. Just as Jacob heard the promise of God, when we open the Scriptures and listen to the Word of God, faith arises in us.

"I committed many sins; I am a deceitful, filthy human being; I am a lustful, riotous human, but Jesus received all the punishment in my place, for a person like me. Thus, my sins are washed away. I am as white as snow. Jesus truly loved me and did not spare His own life. Jesus is truly a precious person."

When God recorded the Scriptures through His servants, He did so in order for the heart, "Ah, that's right. My sins are surely washed away. I do not have sins," would naturally arise inside of us. Therefore, if you do not listen to the voice of Satan, do not follow your thoughts, and most carefully listen to the voice of God in the Scriptures, faith becomes clearly developed in your heart.

But just as what Esau saw differed from what Jacob saw, another heart arises in us when we listen to the humanistic voice of Satan.

"I committed so many sins, and Jesus was crucified, but my sins probably are not all washed away. How could I dare say I don't have sins? I have my conscience. I cannot say that I am righteous."

That is where our hearts are constantly inclined to when we listen to Satan's voice. I can truly feel this deeply as I give spiritual counseling and preach the Word.

"Ah, this person has deeper humanistic thoughts than the Word of God. He listens to the sounds of his conscience more than the voice of God."

Loving folks, just as Adam and Eve heard the Word of God in Eden, but also heard the words of the serpent, there are always two voices you hear when you are living spiritual life. The people who followed the voice of Satan were all destroyed and cursed. Even now, Satan says many things inside of us. Sometimes he even speaks to us through our conscience. There are many who think that the conscience is a good thing. In some ways the conscience appears to be good, but if the conscience deviates from the Word of God, it, too, is something that is not good. Even though we believe that Jesus died for our sins, if we do not simply listen to the voice of God but to our own voice as well, it seems that our sins remain as they were even though Jesus was crucified. That is why people cannot say they have no sin and can only say humanistic things, like, "I am a sinner who has committed sins."

What did the Word of God say?

*For all have sinned, and have come short of the glory of God; Being justified freely by his grace, through the redemption that is in Christ Jesus;* (Romans 3:23-24)

The Word of God says that we are righteous. Within Abraham; within Joseph; and within David, Satan put thoughts that were completely opposite of the promise after they had received the promise. In you, as well, the Word of God and the thoughts planted in you by Satan are both at work. Now listen to the word and voice of God like Jacob, and remove the parts that are not of the Word of God from your heart. If your heart dwells in the promise of God, you become people of faith, and God will work in you greatly through the power of the Holy Spirit.

# 40

## *Leah and Rachel*

*And Laban had two daughters: the name of the elder was Leah, and the name of the younger was Rachel. Leah was tender eyed; but Rachel was beautiful and well favoured. And Jacob loved Rachel; and said, I will serve thee seven years for Rachel thy younger daughter.* (Genesis 29:16~18)

## The Process of the Heart Developing

We can see when we read the Bible that it talks about the world of the heart of man. Whether a humble and meek heart is developed in man, or an arrogant, wicked, and rugged heart is formed in man, there is a certain process involved for these hearts to be formed. These hearts are formed by this process. You cannot become humble or meek through your own effort. Then, how do our hearts become arrogant and how do they become humble? The Bible precisely shows us the image of our hearts becoming humbled in order to lead us to humbleness because we cannot understand these things alone. On the other hand, Satan constantly leads us to become arrogant and hardened.

What we are going to talk about today clearly shows us how man's heart develops. Jacob was living at the house of his uncle, Laban. One day, Laban said, "Because you are my brother, should you therefore serve me for nothing? What should your wages be?" Laban had two daughters: Leah, who was the elder one, and Rachel, who was the younger one. Leah was tender-eyed while Rachel was lovely and beautiful. Do you know what happens to women's personalities when their faces are lovely and beautiful? Often, one's personality is influenced by the people around you. People around women with lovely and beautiful faces recognize that they are beautiful. When a difficult feat is accomplished by a woman with a lovely and beautiful face, people say that what she did was heroic. However, when the same feat is done by a woman who is not so beautiful, the same people say that she must have been bitter. In addition, even though women with lovely and beautiful faces make mistakes, they are often looked upon forgivingly and their wrongdoings mostly overlooked or easily dismissed. Thus, women with beautiful faces naturally become proud and arrogant. They become unable to understand the hearts of others and are more likely to live self-centered lives.

It is that you are not carefully observant of these things. If a woman with a lovely, beautiful face has a humble personality, she becomes a tremendously radiant person. However, people for the most part become proud and arrogant if they are a bit more lovely and beautiful than others. Because people are more understanding toward them, it becomes extremely difficult for them to bend their will, break themselves, or humble themselves. On the contrary, women with not so beautiful faces easily have their blemishes revealed with the slightest of mistakes. Thus, they are easily able to control and break themselves. This is how character is built.

## Leah, Who Entered Jacob's Bridal Room

Of Laban's two daughters, Leah was tender-eyed, while Rachel was lovely and beautiful. Which of the two would Jacob want to marry? Needless to say, it was the lovely and beautiful Rachel he wanted to marry. Jacob tells Laban, "I will serve you seven years for Rachel your younger daughter." Back then it was common for relatives to marry one another. Laban then makes a promise, saying, "Fine. It is better that I give her to you than to another man. I will give you Rachel if you serve me seven years."

Now Rachel and Jacob were in love. However, Leah, who should be marrying first because she is the older daughter, thinks of Rachel who will marry first. This makes Leah contemplate and have much time to reflect upon how weak she is.

This was how the seven years passed, and Jacob finally married and decorated his bridal room. Surely, Jacob was supposed to marry Rachel, but that night, Laban told Leah to enter into the bridal room instead of Rachel. At that time, it was dark in the bridal room and one would not be able to tell who the bride was. Even so, Leah was dumbfounded. Jacob hates her and loves Rachel; this was something that completely went against her pride. She also thought, "Is this okay to do?" Most women would say, "Father, I would rather not get married if this is how it's going to be. I will not do this. I know Jacob loves Rachel. I may be able to spend a night with him, but he will see me in the morning and hate me. I will forever be despised and treated with contempt. How could I go through with this? I'd rather get old as a virgin. I cannot do this."

However, Leah knew that she was ugly and lacking. She was not accustomed to exerting her opinions or perceptions. She was accustomed to denying herself and followed her father's words.

## From a Life of Rachel to a Life of Leah

I lived like Rachel. It was not that I was great that I lived like Rachel. Although one is pitiful, if he thinks of himself as being great, then he lives like Rachel. Even if a person is foolish, if he thinks that he is smart then he is number one in his own heart. Even if a person is pitiful, if he thinks he is great then he is that way in his own heart. For a long time, I lived spiritual life like Rachel. I thought I was great and I thought I was smart and I thought I was better than others. Thus, it was difficult for me to break my heart, and I often became upset when my suggested opinions were not accepted by my friends. Therefore, I always tried to break the opinions of others. Everything I wanted had to be adhered to, things had to go according to my will, everything I wanted to be done. . . . So it was only natural that my friends did not like me much.

One day, I received the tremendous grace of God to have an opportunity to see myself. Before, when I saw myself with my own eyes, I thought I was great and smart. But when I saw myself through the eyes God gave me, I was such a filthy, evil, dirty, foul, deceitful, and pitiful human being. Not only in theory, but I came to realize this deeply in my heart. After this, I looked upon my past. All the things I thought I did well and thought were going to go well, after some time, they did not work out. Ten out of ten and a hundred out of a hundred times they were all failures. However, I did not even know that. I only thought, "How did that happen? I did a good job. . . ."

By the grace of God, I was able to come down from Rachel's position to that of Leah. After coming down to Leah's position, after becoming a pitiful person who can do nothing, the Word of God entered my heart exactly as it was.

## The Reason Leah Could Have Her Heart

Leah's pride would not allow her to enter the bridal room when Jacob wanted to marry her younger sister.

"Father, Jacob loves Rachel. I may spend a night with him, but what will I do when he wakes up in the morning and sees me? Father, just let Rachel get married. I'm just going to live by myself." This is what most women would say and come to decide. However, Leah was different.

"Leah!"

"Yes, Father."

"Go into Jacob's room tonight and sleep there."

"Yes, Father, I will."

Leah could have this heart because she had emptied herself. When we look at the steps or paths the greats of the Bible took in their lives, there were no contentions or individual opinions in them. Why did they live this way? It was because they knew themselves precisely. For everything they do is a failure, ruined, and knew that they cannot do anything, they could no longer exalt themselves and exert their opinions. Now they were accepting the thoughts of someone who was greater than they were.

The most difficult thing in spiritual life today for many people is just that. When their thoughts and the Word of God are complete opposites, without hesitation, they should throw their thoughts away and follow the Word of God. However, the problem is that this is easier said than done. The Lord says, "It is better to give than to receive," but people think of receiving to be more blessed. The Lord says, "He that is abased will be exalted and he who is exalted will be abased." However, people think that they have to push down and step on others to stand exalted. Many people live spiritual life with such thoughts. Therefore, it is not a problem when your thoughts and God's thoughts do not differ, but problems in spiritual life arise because you are unable to break your thoughts and follow the Lord's thoughts when they differ from one another. I don't think there is a problem other than this.

Thus, God continually humbles our hearts. Whether you have an ugly face, are crippled, have mental disabilities, have made mistakes, or have committed crimes, through all of these things, God moves you from the position of Rachel to the position of Leah. God leads you from a world of living in your own greatness, with your own opinions, into a world where you can only deny yourself. If you are someone who can think deeply, and deeply reflect upon yourself, you can only feel that you can only do so much even if you do well. You can see that in your business, or in rearing your children, just how truly lacking you are.

## I Thought I Could Rear My Children Well

Before I was married, I made up my mind to rear my children well whenever I would become married and have children. When I saw children who were disorderly, I often thought, "How can his parents rear their kid like that?" But who would want to rear their children to be disorderly? Everyone wants to rear their children well, but it does not work out so well, and I had never considered that. I thought parents who had misbehaving children did so because they did not have the heart to rear their children properly. So I thought that I could rear my children properly if I just tried to. But after becoming married and having children myself, I one day came home late after witnessing, and saw that my daughter's hand was completely wrapped in bandages.

"Honey, why is Eun-sook's hand wrapped in bandages?"

My daughter had gone over to a neighbor's house to play, when one of the children pushed my daughter. Houses in the countryside, a long time ago, had small doors that went from the room to the kitchen. My daughter fell through that door and landed on top of the charcoal furnace. Her hands and buttocks were burnt, and it broke my heart. I held my sleeping daughter and prayed to God.

"God, allow Eun-sook not to be scarred and please heal her quickly."

During my prayer, I remembered my determination to rear my kids well.

"You live in the same house as your loving daughter, but what did you do for her when she was falling on top of the charcoal furnace?"

I was completely powerless although my daughter was hurt. To think that I could rear my daughter straight was nonsensical, and it was a tremendously arrogant heart.

"God, I was so arrogant. God, with what power can I protect my daughter from danger, and how can I rear her well? I cannot do it. God, I am not confident in rearing my children so I leave them in your hands. You rear them."

I see many parents who are worried and tormented because of their problematic children. What parents would want to rear their children to be this way? They suffer, cry, and are saddened because it is not going according to their will. If it went according to their will, why would they cry? I so recklessly thought that I could rear my children properly only if I made up my mind to. I realized deeply in my heart how foolish that thought was the day my daughter was hurt. Thus, I turned my heart around before God.

I thought that I can do anything in most instances and lived with a heart like that of Rachel. Because I thought of myself as smart and great, I had the heart, "These are things from man, so why couldn't I do them?" But in reality, there was nothing I could do. God taught me in many aspects about this.

"There is nothing I can do!"

"I can do it. I only need to pray. I only need to not sin and live spiritual life. What is the problem?"

I can easily have this heart when I have the heart to believe in myself. However, if God does not help me, it is such an ignorant and arrogant thought to think that I can live according to the Scriptures, do good things, and please God. Who skips a tithe because he wants to? Who sins because he wants to? Satan has deceived us to make us into Rachel.

## Though It Seems Rachel Is Happy and Leah Is Miserable

There was a great commotion the morning after Leah entered Jacob's bridal room and slept with him.

"You! Why are you here?"

Jacob almost fainted.

"I slept with you last night? Oh, no! Get out!"

Jacob was angry and went to Laban and yelled at him.

"I served you seven years for your younger daughter, Rachel. Why did you give me Leah? How can you do this to me?"

This must have torn Leah's heart apart. Laban spoke.

"It must not be done so in our country, to give the younger before the first-born. But serve seven more years. I will give you Rachel as well after seven years."

Jacob married Rachel because he wanted her, and Leah was given as an additive. Now it seemed that Rachel would be happy and Leah would be miserable. However, since Leah knew herself deeply, she sought God while Rachel lived without God because she was well in every aspect. Time passed and in the latter parts of Genesis chapter 29, it talks about Leah having sons.

*And when the Lord saw that Leah was hated, he opened her womb: but Rachel was barren. And Leah conceived, and bare a son, and she called his name Reuben. . . .* (Genesis 29:31-32)

Leah had a second son and called him, Simeon. She called her third son, Levi, and her fourth son, Judah. Reuben means, "Behold, a son!" How happy she must have been to have sons! Leah was tender-eyed and was a woman with nothing to exalt, but she gained hope from God. Simeon means, "God has heard." Levi means, "unity," signifying that her husband will now unite with her for she has bore three sons. Judah means, "praise," which says she praises God who has given her sons. Since Leah had faith, she had hope and was able to have sons.

But, Rachel became angry at Jacob because she was not

being able to have children.

"Give me children, or else I will die!"

She is railing with her own methods because she is arrogant. When even this did not work, she said, "Then enter into my maid and have a son through her." The name of the son who was born through this was Dan. Dan means, "God has judged me." Then she had a second son through the maid. This son was named, Naphtali, which means that she competed with her sister and won. Because she has no faith in her heart, these are the only kinds of names she can give to her sons.

## God Who Leads Us to Be like Leah

People of faith make the things they face, regardless of what they are, into opportunities to give thanks and praise and opportunities to unite with God and have hope. Since Leah has nothing to boast of, she cannot rely on herself, but on God. This caused faith to arise in her heart towards God. Therefore, regardless of what she faced, she accepted them as joy, thankfulness, and hope. Rachel was completely different. She had a grudge: "I won the competition," and was rugged, and had evil things come from her heart.

Rachel was loved by people because she had a pretty face. Because of this, she did not have any opportunity to break her heart or discover her true image. Therefore, she even made her children tools to fulfill her ambitions. Because Leah was an ugly and despised woman, she could deeply look upon herself and humble her heart. She looked to God and had children through the grace of God. When we see her sons' names, we see that her heart was overflowing with hope and joy.

God gives you pain, blemishes, and weaknesses to guide you to break and humble yourself like Leah. We need to have a heart like that of Leah, but Satan exalts our great aspects to make us arrogant and to make us into people who, by our ambitions, like Rachel, are unable to receive the grace of God.

There may be great or smart people among you, but if you have the eyes to see yourself deeply, you can feel how lacking you are before God. If you could truly see how you are lacking and throw away your ambition and your thoughts, you, too, can have faith and become people who receive the grace of God.

# 41

## *Jacob's Scheme and the Blessing of God*

*And the angel of God spake unto me in a dream, saying, Jacob: And I said, Here am I. And he said, Lift up now thine eyes, and see, all the rams which leap upon the cattle are ringstraked, speckled, and grisled: for I have seen all that Laban doeth unto thee. I am the God of Bethel, where thou anointedst the pillar, and where thou vowedst a vow unto me: now arise, get thee out from this land, and return unto the land of thy kindred.* (Genesis 31:11-13)

## Jacob's Scheme

Jacob went to Laban's house, married Leah and Rachel, had children, and herded Laban's cattle. Time passed and Jacob said that he would go home. Then Laban said, "You decide your wage. I will give you your wage." Jacob said, "I will not ask for anything, but if cattle that are ring-streaked, speckled or spotted are born, uncle, those shall be mine, and have all the white sheep yours. Then I will herd your cattle." Laban saw that most sheep were white and not ring-streaked and spotted, rejoiced and agreed to do so. That day, Laban removed the ring-streaked, spotted and speckled sheep from his flock and left them to his son, and then had Jacob herd the rest of the flock.

Jacob continued to herd Laban's flock. The interesting thing is, Jacob saw that the sheep mated at the creek where they drank. Thus Jacob came up with a scheme and took the rods of green poplar, hazel, and chestnut trees and pilled them to make white streaks in them. Then he mixed them with green branches and made them mottled. Then he laid these before the sheep when they would mate and when the sheep brought forth offspring, they had ring-streaked, speckled, and spotted young. Jacob became very excited. Thus when the stronger sheep would mate he would lay the prepared branches before them and did not do so when the weaker sheep mated. Therefore the stronger would bring forth ring-streaked and speckled sheep, and the weaker sheep brought forth white sheep. Jacob was very excited and thought he was doing well.

But later on, what did God say to him? God had made the rams that brought forth offspring that were all ring-streaked, spotted, and speckled. It was not because Jacob had pilled the rods of green poplar, hazel, and chestnut trees and laid these branches before the sheep when they were mating that ring-streaked, spotted, and speckled sheep were brought forth. It was God who had done this. Jacob did not know this and thought such offspring were brought forth because of what he had done.

## People Who Think Themselves to Be Good

I once asked a doctor if placing pilled branches of poplar, hazel, and chestnut trees that had been mottled in front of sheep would bring about such offspring. The doctor said that that had no basis whatsoever. It was not that Jacob did this that allowed him to gain the speckled, spotted, or ring-streaked offspring, but he thought he had gained by doing what he did.

This is not only true in life, but also true in spiritual life. "I prayed and God blessed me. I witness hard and God protected my life. I was very helpful to others and God blessed me." There are many people who believe this way.

Let us talk about this in detail. There are good people among us and there are also bad people. There is a difference in standard depending on the people, but there are people who are better and there are those who are evil. But this is only to the extent of the standard of man. If measured by the standard of God, no matter how good a person may be, he is only a filthy, dirty, pitiful, and evil person. If you think God gives punishment because you have done evil, there would be no one on earth who could stay alive.

Let's think about it. Do you sin only once or twice? Do you commit wickedness once or twice? Do you lie once or twice? Do you go against the Word of God once or twice? Most people do not have their standard upon God but upon the wicked, so even if they are committing wickedness, they see themselves as better than the wicked. Even in spiritual life, people who base their standard on those whose spiritual life is a mess for the most part think, "That person is so pious. He acts like he has so much faith when he comes to church, but do you know how wicked he is out in the world? At least I am not like him. I do sin, but I did not put a nail through Jesus' heart."

People think that they are blessed because they have been good and truthful. On the other hand, there are many people who think, "What sin did I commit that you are giving me this hardship, God?" when going through difficulties. When difficulties arise, in the beginning they don't know what to do, then think about it when there is some quiet time. There are so many people who think, "I did not live wickedly. I lived as a good person. What did I do wrong that God is doing this to me?" People do not know themselves precisely. It is because God is graceful, merciful, and good, and it is because God bestows His grace unto us that we can live as we do. If God punished us each time we sinned; if God repaid us for all the sins we committed, there is no one among us who could stay alive.

In addition, people who think they have done good are only good by their own standards. There are many people who say, "I grew up always being called good." But the funny thing is which passing adult doesn't call children good? If you say hello well once, adults say, "Oh, you are a good boy," and give compliments for the smallest deed. So who doesn't grow up hearing compliments? But the fact that they have been called good remains for a long time in their heart.

When I was young, I once finished first in a sprint. From then on I always remembered myself as someone who ran well. Because people remember what they have done well for a long time, no matter who it is, he rates himself better than what he actually is. Therefore it is terribly wrong for you to see yourself with your assessment of yourself. But this is how most want to assess themselves.

## It Is the Grace of God . . .

God allowed Jacob to realize.

*And the angel of God spake unto me in a dream, saying, Jacob: And I said, Here am I. And he said, Lift up now thine eyes, and see, all the rams which leap upon the cattle are ring-streaked, speckled, and grizzled: for I have seen all that Laban doeth unto thee.* (Genesis 31:11-12)

Laban constantly changed the wages using humanistic methods and did not want to give wages to Jacob. Thus God stood on Jacob's side and had the sheep bring forth spotted, speckled, and ring-streaked offspring. Jacob was able to have a lot of cattle and became rich through God. But Jacob thought that such offspring were brought forth because he had pilled the poplar, hazel, and chestnut trees and mottled them and placed these branches before the sheep, bringing forth offspring.

We are just like Jacob. We eat and live through receiving the grace of God but people think that they can eat and live because of their own greatness. If one places first in a contest, that, too, is through the grace of God, but he thinks that it is because of his own greatness that he won first place. Suppose I practiced the violin until my neck was bruised, my arms cramped, and the strings on my bow were all torn and I finished in first place. But can I perform if my arm is broken? Suppose you became confused in your thoughts. If you cannot concentrate during your performance, your performance will be broken up. Of these many things, if just one thing goes wrong, the performances cannot be successful.

As a pastor, I am so thankful that I can stand at the pulpit of our church each Sunday morning and give a sermon. I once said, "I am so thankful that I can stand at the pulpit," and one brother replied, "What is that to be thankful about? Isn't that something natural for you, Pastor?" I then said, "What are you talking about? So many conditions have to be met for me to be able to stand at the pulpit. I cannot stand if my legs break, I cannot stand if I become weak, I cannot stand if I have nothing to preach about, I cannot stand if there is no one to listen,

I cannot stand. . . ." There are many preachers who quit along the way. At one point they used to preach spiritual words, and some quit after one year, some after five years, and some after ten years. . . . That is why it is so funny to say that I could keep the pulpit. If God takes away wisdom today, if He removes the Word from me, what will I preach and what would I talk about? I become someone who is absolutely nothing.

Even in doing business in the world, there are so many instances where able and smart people one day become bankrupt, or become diseased and fail. Often well-known companies have to close overnight. People think that they are doing something well because they are great, but that is actually not so.

## Why Were the Days of His Years Evil?

God shows us the world of the heart from Genesis. Later in Jacob's life, he finds out that Joseph has become governor and goes down to Egypt and stands before Pharaoh king of Egypt. Pharaoh asks Jacob, "How old are you?" Right then Jacob says, "I am one hundred thirty. I have not attained the years of my fathers, yet few and evil have the days of the years of my life been."

Jacob went through evil years because he was always scheming. When Jacob was in his mother's womb, the two children were fighting inside the womb and their mother, Rebekah, prayed to God. Right then God said this:

"Two great nations are within you. Two manner of people shall be separated from your womb. One people shall be stronger than the other people, and the elder shall serve the younger."

God selected Jacob from the mother's womb to be blessed. But Jacob sought out to be blessed through using human methods such as buying his older brother's birthright with a bowl of pottage of lentils. These humanistic methods and means made Jacob fall into emptiness and put him through rough days and years. Jacob was smarter and was sharper than anyone else. Therefore with that wisdom he always lived using human methods. Jacob trusted his own methods and means. God would even have provided a wife for him, but he felt, "Rachel is pretty. I'd better make Rachel my wife," in his heart. Therefore he tried to marry Rachel, but out of nowhere he spent the first night with Leah. God permitted this to happen to Jacob.

How does God lead us? We can never reach the standard of God through our wisdom or methods. We can realize salvation when the wisdom of God comes upon us. The power of God must come for us to defeat sin. We must receive the grace of God for us to become holy and righteous. All of this happens through God, but we trust in our own power. I will keep the Ten Commandments, I will be faithful, I will not sin, and I will try to do good. God knows that this will not work and tells us not to do this, but we think that things will go well through our own intelligence and wisdom. We think that all things are accomplished through ourselves, but this is so foolish.

## God Who Makes You Fail

God made us unable to keep the law to have us realize our true image. Who can keep the law? There is no one who can keep the law. God has made you unable to live a life that pleases Him. Therefore, He crumbles down your heart to believe in yourself. When the faith to believe in yourself crumbles down, the faith to believe in God begins to arise in you.

It is impossible for me to reach the seat of blessing through doing good, my righteousness, keeping the law, and serving God well. One should be blessed not through himself but through the faith to believe in God. To have this faith, you have to give up on yourself. For this, God had you fail. Even though you grind your teeth and make up your mind to not sin and live a life of pleasing God, it does not work. Isn't that so? You have failed.

"God, now I will keep the law! From today I will not sin!"

Today there are countless church goers who become determined and make up their minds. That is exactly like Peter's determination when he said, "Though they all deny you, I will not deny you, Lord! Though I die with you, I will never deny you!" Everyone, did Peter do as he was determined to? He did not. It did not go according to how he had determined. God did not allow it. If things do go according to people's determination, they would all believe in themselves. People who believe in themselves cannot believe in God.

True spiritual life is made of "repentance" and "faith." Repentance is not merely confessing, "I committed theft. I committed adultery." It is saying, "I had believed in myself. I absolutely should not trust myself! I am not worthy of being trusted! I am weak, evil, and dirty!" and turning from trusting yourself. Then you can believe in God. Turning from yourself to the side of believing in God, that is true repentance.

## Who Can Make Me Fall if God Establishes Me?

Jacob trusted his schemes. He believed his methods and trusted his ways. Therefore God made all the things he did turn into pain. When he was in his mother's womb, God already had Jacob be blessed through the promise, "The elder shall serve the younger." Jacob, through his scheme, tried to be blessed but thought that his older brother would kill him, making him run away to Padan-aram. Everything Jacob did was this way. He tried to marry Rachel but he ended up marrying Leah first. He tried to increase his wealth through scheming when the sheep mated but later found out it was a blessing from God.

Before Jacob realized this, he trusted himself and thought he could do everything with his methods. But later on he says, "Evil have the days of my years been." People of faith all go through this process. Abraham also tried to have a son through human effort and had Ishamel. Later on, he realized his methods were useless, then had Isaac through faith in God. We, too, must go through that process in spiritual life. Most people believe in themselves and rather than expecting what God will accomplish for them, they try to reach the standard of God through their own effort. That is so foolish in the eyes of God.

Loving folks, isn't it so? Don't you trust yourself and are trying to do something before God? That is so foolish. You have to completely throw yourself away and rely on God because we cannot reach God through our methods. We cannot wash our sins away, but God has to wash them for us to be clean. Our lives do not become clean through our effort or determination but we can live a clean life through God cleansing us. God has to make me prosperous for me to be so, and for me to be holy God has to make me so. All of this is not done through our determination or resolve, but people do not know this and rely on their determination, effort, and resolve. There are so many people living spiritual life this way.

If you hold onto God, Satan can quickly make you let go. It is because Satan is stronger than we are. But if God holds us, who can make His hands let go? No one can. If you rely on yourself, you can easily fall over, but if God establishes you, who could make you fall? If God sanctifies you, if God justifies you, if God cleanses you, if God blesses you, who can make these fall? Putting hope in God is true faith.

# 42

# *Jacob Who Wrestled and Prevailed Against God*

*And Jacob said, O God of my father Abraham, and God of my father Isaac, the LORD which saidst unto me, Return unto thy country, and to thy kindred, and I will deal well with thee:* (Genesis 32:9)

## Your Older Brother Is Bringing 400 Soldiers with Him

Genesis chapter 32 chronicles the process of Jacob going from Mahanaim to Peniel. Mahanaim means, "the hosts of God," and Peniel means, "the face of God." Mahanaim represents how God starts to be with us once we receive salvation, and Peniel represents us standing before God upon finishing our lives. In other words, it can be said that Genesis chapter 32 has summarized our lives after receiving salvation.

As you know, Jacob stole the birthright from his older brother, Esau, in Canaan and then also stole Esau's blessing. Esau then tried to kill him for doing so and Jacob fled to Padan-aram, to his uncle's house, to elude Esau. Jacob gained wives and many children as well as much cattle and wealth during his 20 years in Padan-aram. Genesis chapter 32 is about the process of Jacob taking all of these things and returning to Canaan, his homeland.

On his way to his homeland, Jacob wondered, "Esau tried to kill me when I was leaving home. It's been 20 years, and I wonder how he feels now. Has his bitterness toward me been resolved? When I return, will he welcome me joyfully? Or, will he go against me and try to kill me?" Jacob wanted to know Esau's heart, and therefore sent people ahead to salute him and let Esau know that he was coming. But these people returned to Jacob and said, "Lord, your older brother is coming this way with 400 soldiers." It was not much of a problem that the older brother was coming to see him, but when he heard that he was bringing 400 men with him, Jacob was terrified. "There is vengeance still in my brother's heart! It's been 20 years, but he is coming to destroy me!" Since he thought that his brother would destroy his people and all his cattle, Jacob was extremely anguished and afraid.

## The Two Methods of Jacob

What do you do in your spiritual life when something terrifying happens? What methods do you seek? Herein shows the difference between those with faith and those without faith. Anyone can attend church service, pray, and read the Bible when things are normal. But when we face difficulties or pain we cannot solve on our own, how we go about taking care of them is important. We can see Jacob going toward these problems with two methods.

The first method is him looking to the promise of God. Jacob met God at Bethel before he went to Padan-aram. Right then, God promised, "Jacob, I am the God of your father, Abraham, the God of your father, Isaac, and I am your God. I will be with you and your children. Your children shall be many like the dust of the earth. I will be with you and protect you wherever you go, and I will not leave you until I bring you again to this land."

Now if Jacob has the faith to believe in the promise of God, he would feel, "God said He will protect me, and He said that all the tribes of the earth will be blessed through my seed. So God will protect me. He will help me." Then Jacob would have said, "So what is the problem if my older brother, Esau, is bringing 400 men with him? Even if it were 4,000 or 40,000 men, what problem is that? It is not a problem at all since God is protecting me." He would not have any fear if he had the clear faith to believe in God.

God helped Jacob till now, and clearly told him in Padan-aram, "Go to your homeland to your kindred. I will bestow grace onto thee." It was clear that God would not leave Jacob to be killed. If Jacob has the faith to believe in that promise, there is nothing for Jacob to be afraid of. However, Jacob was not close with God as he lived in Padan-aram and in his heart he thought, "Will the promise that God made be kept? Will God help me?"

*Then Jacob was greatly afraid, and distressed: and he divided the people that was with him, and the flocks, and the herds, and the camels, into two bands; And said, If Esau come to the one company, and smite it, then the other company which is left shall escape. And Jacob said, O God of my father Abraham, and God of my father Isaac, the Lord which saidst unto me, Return unto thy country, and to thy kindred, and I will deal well with thee.* (Genesis 32:7-9)

Although Jacob says that God promised to protect him, he was trembling in fear. Thus, Jacob arranged for one company to be able to escape if his brother, Esau, were to strike. He also hid the sons of his wives in the back and put forth the sons of the concubines, such as Dan and Naphtali, in the front. He still had no peace even though he was praying to God, so he thought, "Ah, let us first give presents to my brother." He then prepared 200 female goats, 20 male goats, 200 ewes, 20 rams, 30 milch camels, 40 kine, 10 bulls, 20 female asses, and 10 foals. He wanted to melt his brother's heart through giving him all this cattle. Jacob was using this second method, which was a humanly one.

## How Will You Stand Before the Face of God?

Let's think about the two methods Jacob prepared. Even if one company runs away while the other is struck, that company will also be killed. In addition, Esau is bringing 400 soldiers. If one company does run away, with all the children, women, and cattle, how far could they actually go? This plan looks useless to us, but Jacob used this method. He also prepared presents to melt the heart of his brother, Esau, but what good would presents be when his brother was coming to kill him?

When we look at these facts, the faith to believe in God's promise is what's actually important. When he looks to God, since God promised that He would protect and care for him, it could only be that way. However, since he could not believe and rely on the promise, we see that Jacob was in fear and distress. This is very heartbreaking.

Such things happen often in our spiritual life as well. When you arrive at Peniel; when you come to see the face of God, you also will try to come before God in two ways. There will be some people who come forth before God through holding on to the promise God made them. There will also be another type of people who bring forth what man has done. "I tithed. I built a chapel. I prayed all night long. I fasted and prayed. I gave much offering. I helped orphans. . . ." You cannot bring forth both the promise God made you and what you have done for God. You can only bring one, but which one of the two brings peace to your heart? It is only the promise of God.

God said that He clearly keeps His promise to us. That God promised Jacob, "I will protect you no matter where you go, and I will not leave you until you return to this land."

If Jacob believes the promise, he will think in his heart, "Esau is bringing 400 men, but God said He will protect me. God will protect me from my brother. This is absolutely clear. God does not lie. Therefore, even if my brother was bringing not only 400, but 4,000 or 40,000 men, I am safe. There is nothing for me to worry about." Nevertheless, if he does not have that faith, he says, "If Esau strikes down one company, then the other will run away," and uses the human method of giving presents to his older brother. For the moment, this appears to be good, but it is absolutely useless in front of God.

Just as Jacob was this way, our spiritual lives are also like this. We will one day stand before God. Suppose you stand before God tonight. Suppose you had cancer and the doctor said, "You now only have one day to live." Then you will begin to think, "I will stand before God tonight! Then how will I stand before Him? I had sinned much till now and I have been faithful in many other things. . . . God will accept me since I gave much offering and prayed much."

There are many who think this way.

## I Was in Prison for 14 Years for Jesus, and I Can't Go to Heaven?

I once met a pastor of an underground church when I visited Vietnam. I spoke to him about spiritual life and I asked him a question.

"Pastor, can you go to heaven?"

"Yes, I can go to heaven," he replied.

"How can you go?"

"I was locked in prison for 14 years for the Lord. Since I was in prison for 14 years for the Lord, don't you think God would let me into heaven?"

I laughed.

"Pastor, you cannot go to heaven through your works. Works will not do."

Then this pastor's face turned red and he began to angrily ask me questions.

"What? Pastor! Have you seen anyone who suffered as much as I have to believe in God? Pastor, do you know me so well that you are saying such things? Do you think I was the only one who suffered in prison? My wife was tormented and called in for questioning every day. My son lived like a beggar out on the streets. That's how we lived for 14 years. This was how I lived, and I can't go to heaven? I can't go to heaven? Then who can go to heaven?"

I opened the Bible.

"Ephesians chapter 2 says, 'For by grace are ye saved, through faith; and that not of yourselves: it is the gift of God: Not of works, lest any man should boast.' The Bible says that salvation is not through what we have done. It does not say that salvation is through our works. Salvation has nothing to do with how well or poorly we do."

This pastor did not know what to say. He became upset and said, "I will no longer speak to you," and ran outside. It really broke my heart to see this.

## We Must Look to the Promise of God

Everyone, if we could do this and that for Jesus and enter into heaven with our good deeds, then why would God send Jesus to die for us? Why would God have Jesus crucified? Because it could not be done through us; because it could not be done through our efforts and labor, no matter what good, righteous, or honest things we may do, God sent Jesus. We are able to stand before God not because of our deeds, but through Jesus.

"I gave all my wealth to Jesus. I went to prison for Jesus. I allowed my body to be burnt for Jesus. . . ." You cannot go to heaven with what you have done, no matter what it may be.

We must look to the promise of God. Because our works or efforts cannot do, God sent Jesus to have Him be crucified to forgive all of our sins. Then God made a promise. God said to the Israelites in Exodus chapter 12, "I will pass over you when I see the blood of the lamb." He did not say that He will pass over upon seeing the good they have done. The night the angel, going from house to house, killed all the first-born with a sword, in which houses did he enter to bring the judgment of death upon the first-borns? The day the fearful judgment of the first-borns came upon all of Egypt, what did the angel have to see to not pass judgment but pass over? It says that when he sees the blood, he will pass over.

We have to believe this promise God made.

"God, I have many sins. I was not good, and lived an evil, filthy, and dirty life. God, you promised that when you see the blood of Jesus Christ who was crucified for my sins, the blood of the lamb, you will pass over me. Jesus was crucified and shed His blood for my sins."

God then sees the blood of Jesus and accepts us.

Unfortunately, people take the Word of God and the promise of God lightly, and they value what they have done. Therefore, their hearts are always insecure. At first it seems they are able to do good but not long after it falls apart, and falls apart again. It seems that they are able to keep the law a little, but they break the law again and again. They live sinning every day and cannot help but feel insecure in coming before God.

## You Wrestled with God and Prevailed

Jacob tried to go to Esau with his own method. Jacob had two ways: the promise of God and his own way. But Jacob was afraid because he had no faith to believe in the promise although he spoke of it. Therefore, he brought forth his method. One company would run away if the other was struck. He lined up the sons of the concubines first, then the sons of Leah, then the sons of Rachel, and prepared presents for his older brother. But these could not bring true peace to Jacob's heart.

Now his men and cattle were all crossing the Jabbok ford, but Jacob was so afraid he couldn't cross it. That night, Jacob wrestled with an angel. Jacob collided with God and sought Him.

"God, bless me! Give me your blessing!"

"What is your name?"

"My name is Jacob."

"You will no longer be called Jacob. You will be called Israel. You wrestled with God and prevailed."

How did Jacob prevail against God? He now believed in the promise of God. Afterwards, when Jacob was passing Peniel, the sun rose.

## God, Didn't You Make the Promise?

Loving folks, we prevail against God when we go forward, believing in His promise because God can never break His promise. But when we go forth with our goodness and our good deeds we always fall into fear.

What kind of a spiritual life do you have? Oftentimes people try to bring forth to God the good they have done and try to stand with that. Do not bring those forth, but go forth looking to Jesus Christ. I hope you will go forth believing in the promise of God. What did God promise us in Hebrews?

*And their sins and iniquities will I remember no more. Now where remission of these is, there is no more offering for sin.* (Hebrews 10:17-18)

Rather than bringing forth the thousands, or tens of thousands of the good you have done when you stand before God, it is most perfect to go forth with just one thing: the promise.

"God, didn't you say that you will not remember my sins?"

If God says that He does not remember them, He does not remember them.

*I have blotted out, as a thick cloud, thy transgressions, and as a cloud, thy sins: return unto me; for I have redeemed thee.* (Isaiah 44:22)

Didn't God promise that He has blotted out our sins like a thick cloud, like the fog that disappears?

*For all have sinned, and come short of the glory of God; Being justified freely by his grace, through the redemption that is in Christ Jesus:* (Romans 3:23-24)

Didn't God call us justified?

We have all sinned. We have all done wickedly before God. This is true of every single person. Therefore, we cannot go to God with the good we have done. Going this way could only be fearful and shameful.

We, like Jacob, can go before God with the promise. Jacob told God, "God, didn't you say that you will give me grace? Protect me and give me grace as you have said!" It is looking to the promise. It is holding onto the promise God made and coming before Him.

Loving folks, it is always insecure and fearful to go before God with our works. Sometimes you may feel you have done well, but afterwards, you see it is nothing but shamefulness. When you throw all of your works away and say, "God, I have many sins. But didn't you promise me that all my sins are washed away? Didn't you say that you will see the blood and pass over? I have come here believing in that promise," you can most boldly stand before God and be blessed.

# 43

# *Thy Name Shall Be Called Israel*

*And he said, Let me go, for the day breaketh. And he said, I will not let thee go, except thou bless me. And he said unto him, What is thy name? And he said, Jacob. And he said, Thy name shall be called no more Jacob, but Israel: for as a prince hast thou power with God and with men, and hast prevailed.* (Genesis 32:26-28)

## Jacob's Method

As we talked about last time, Jacob became very afraid upon hearing that his brother Esau was bringing 400 men with him. He thought, "How am I going to stop my older brother, Esau?" and divided his family and cattle into companies, saying, "If he strikes one, the other will get away." Then he prayed to God. "God, didn't you say that you will protect me? Didn't you say that you will bestow grace upon me?" Still he had no peace or freedom in his heart, and then he tried to melt his brother's heart through preparing gifts to give Esau. Jacob used these methods but these human methods could not bring peace to his heart.

That is how spiritual life always is. Many think, "I will do some good. I will do better to come before God," but people are always afraid, insecure, and uneasy when standing before God through these things. The only way for us to stand before God is to rely on the clear promise of God. Because God does not lie, if Jacob relied on what God promised He would do and came before Him, this is the safest way and it would bring about the most peace in his heart.

## Jacob Who Became Israel

On his way to the land of Canaan, Jacob came to the ford of Jabbok. He needed to cross this river, but he was afraid to cross it. If his older brother, Esau, brought 400 men and attacked him, it would be difficult for him to get away if he has already crossed the river. Therefore, Jacob first had all his people cross while he remained behind by himself. In verse 22,

*And he rose up that night, and took his two wives, and his two women-servants, and his eleven sons, and passed over the ford Jabbok.*

Jacob crossed the ford at night because he was afraid of crossing and hesitated until it became night. Then when it became night, he had no choice but to cross.

*And he took them, and sent them over the brook, and sent over that he had. And Jacob was left alone.* (Genesis 32:23-24)

Jacob was now alone on the other side of the river.

*And there wrestled a man with him, until the breaking of the day. And when he saw that he prevailed not against him, he touched the hollow of his thigh: and the hollow of Jacob's thigh was out of joint, as he wrestled with him.* (Genesis 32:24-25)

A certain man wrestled with Jacob all night long and when the day was breaking, the man said, "Let me go."

Jacob answered, "I will not let you go, except you bless me."

This man then asked Jacob, "What is your name?"

"Jacob."

"You will no longer be called Jacob, but Israel. For you have wrestled with God and have prevailed."

This is the process of Jacob becoming Israel. Jacob became

Israel not because he did something well. God, by grace, had given him the name Israel.

The name Jacob means, "Grabbed the brother's heel, crooked, bent, and twisted." Calling, "Jacob!" is saying, "Hey you crooked man! You're bent! You're twisted!" But God gave Jacob the name Israel. "Israel" means, "wrestled with God and prevailed." Is it that God does not have strength that He could not defeat Jacob? By grace, God gave Jacob the name Israel. From then on, Jacob was Israel, and the name of the country of Israel is from this name given to Jacob.

## I Am Jacob!

Jacob became Israel. The crooked, bent, twisted, and entangled man Jacob of the past became the new Israel through God. It is not that Jacob straightened his twisted self to become Israel.

This may seem like an ordinary story but it is actually telling us in depth about the world of our spiritual life. I did not know that I was a twisted person. I did not know that I was Jacob. I always thought, "I made mistakes, but I am an okay person. I sinned, but nothing too big. I never did anything that crossed the line too much. I did lie, but who doesn't lie? However, I lived as an honest person." Because I lived that way, I never once said, "I am Jacob." I was just Ock Soo Park; I was never Jacob.

"I truly am a crooked person. I am bent and twisted. I am terribly wrong."

I had never once said this. I did not think that I was crooked.

But I, who claimed not to be crooked, lived a crooked life. It was like a crab claiming not to be a crab, yet walking exactly like one. A crab may think that it can walk upright, but it cannot when it tries to. Although I lived a life of doing evil things, lying, fighting, and making my father worry, I did not precisely know myself and did not think that I was that evil of a person. I always lived thinking in my heart, "I only have to be honest. I only need to keep the law. All I have to do is not sin." With my lips I repeated, "Lord, I'm a sinner," but had never said from the core of my heart, "I am the dirty, filthy, evil Jacob!"

But one day, God bestowed grace upon me. When I look back, I feel that at the time God allowed me to borrow His eyes. Right then I saw myself, not through my eyes which I had been seeing through till now, but through the eyes of God. Do you know how I appeared?

*The heart is deceitful above all things and desperately wicked: who can know it?* (Jeremiah 17:9)

Man seen in the eyes of God and myself seen in the eyes of God were deceitful above all things and desperately wicked. There was nothing as rotten as my heart anywhere in this world. Nothing is as deceitful as my heart; nothing as evil as my heart; and nothing as dirty as my heart. I came to realize this fact in my heart. "Ah! I truly am dirty!"

Right then, for the first time in my heart, I confessed, "God, I am a sinner." Of course I had said that I was a sinner in the past as well. I had thought of myself as someone who did have sin, but not a sinner worthy of being destroyed. However, this time, I came to know, "I am a person whose nature itself is twisted, crooked, and evil." I discovered that I could not become good.

## You Are Israel

Once we realize this, it is important to realize the next step. In my eyes, clearly I was Jacob so I said to God, "God, I am Jacob!" But God was seeing me and calling me Israel. This was so confusing.

"God, how can I be Israel? I am not Israel. I am Jacob! I am a crooked human being. I am a dirty, filthy, and evil human being."

"No. You are Israel. You are Israel!"

"God, how can I be Israel? I am a filthy, evil, and dirty human being."

"You are Israel."

A long time ago, I thought of myself as a good person, but I realized the fact that I am truly a filthy, dirty, and evil human being. But afterwards, God looked at me and clearly said, "You are righteous. Holy. Clean." Ah, this was so hard to believe.

"God, how can I be righteous? How can I be holy and clean? I'm not. I am filthy and dirty."

"No. You are righteous, holy, and clean."

"God, no. . . . No. . . ."

Regardless of who you may be, all people have to go through these two processes. First, they have to realize through the grace of God that, "My nature is dirty! That is why filthy and dirty hearts arise within me!" from thinking that their deeds are good. Second, although they appear as dirty humans in their own eyes, they have to accept the words when God calls them righteous. But it is difficult to accept these words.

"God, I am not righteous. I am full of lies, and am an evil, dirty human being."

However, God calls us righteous.

In spiritual life, everyone must first realize that they are truly dirty and filthy. Next, we have to enter the process of having us, who are dirty and filthy, become righteous. It is difficult for people to realize they are true dirty sinners, and it is difficult to become righteous after becoming sinners. This is because the eyes God sees through and the eyes we see through always differ. People who believe in themselves say this:

"God, how can I be Israel? How can I dare prevail against you? I am afraid, so don't say that to me. I am Jacob. I am crooked. I am filthy and dirty."

But if God calls us righteous, we are righteous. If God calls us holy, we are holy.

## It's Wine Now

Jesus went to the wedding at Cana of Galilee when He was in this world. That feast was in need of wine and Jesus said to the servants, "Fill the waterpots with water." The servants filled six waterpots to the brim with water. Do you know what Jesus then said? "Draw out now and serve to the governor of the feast." It meant that the water had turned into wine. The servants could not understand. "How could this be wine? It's water. I just poured water in."

"Master, this is not wine. It is water. We should not serve water. We will be scolded by the master."

That was what the servants thought. But Jesus said, "No. It's wine. Go serve it." It was surely water in the servants' eyes, but

Jesus was calling it wine.

Everyone, this process has to take place for all those who live spiritual life. When Jacob saw himself, he was truly crooked, bent, and twisted, but God was saying that he wasn't so.

"You are Israel. You are no longer crooked. You are not a twisted man anymore. Now, you are no more Jacob. You will no longer be called Jacob, but Israel."

"God, are you calling me Israel? That makes no sense. How can I prevail against you? I am Jacob. Do you know how many twisted things I've done? I stole my brother's birthright, and deceived Laban. You know, I've done all kinds of things. I am not Israel. I am a crooked person. It's fitting that I'm called Jacob. Call me Jacob, God!"

That must have been Jacob's heart, but God spoke.

"You are no longer Jacob. You are Israel. A little while ago you were a crooked person. You were Jacob, but you are now Israel. Do not call yourself Jacob anymore. You are Israel."

Jesus was saying the exact same thing to the servants of the feast when they thought, "Master, this is not wine. This is water. I poured the water from the well here."

"It's not water anymore. Draw out now and serve it. It's wine now."

## God Who Prepared for Thousands of Years to Call Us Righteous

God is saying the same thing to us.

"It is right that you are a sinner. You lied. You committed wickedness. You hated others. You are a sinner. But now you are righteous!"

*For all have sinned, and come short of the glory of God; Being justified freely by his grace, through the redemption that is in Christ Jesus:* (Romans 3:23-24)

"Now you are righteous!"

God saw Jacob and said, "You are Israel." Jesus saw the water and said, "This is wine." God saw us, the sinners, and said, "You are righteous." Today, many people fight against God.

"God, it is not so. I am a sinner. I have many sins."

I, too, could not believe the Word of God that called me righteous.

"How could I be righteous? I'm afraid to dare call myself righteous. How could I say I have no sins? How could I say I am holy? That's nonsense."

So I read the Bible. I read Genesis, Exodus, Leviticus. . . . As I read the Bible, chapter by chapter, I could see that God had done many things to make us righteous; we who are dirty, evil, and filthy. God did not only say with His lips that He made us righteous, but prepared for thousands of years beforehand to make us righteous. Even in what we are talking about today, as a part of that, God told Abraham, "All of mankind will be blessed through your seed," and that seed represents Jesus.

God sent His son, Jesus, 2,000 years ago to this earth to forgive our sins according to His promise. God could not simply call us righteous. To make us righteous, He had to wash our sins away, and to do so, God had Jesus crucified. Jesus prayed at the village of, Gethsemane, "My Father, if you will, take this cup from me. But not as I will, but the will of the father." God knew that Jesus could not avoid the cup in order to make us righteous and had Jesus crucified.

Jesus shouted, "My God, my God, why have you forsaken me?" at the cross. God forsook Jesus once. Why did He do so? It was because Jesus was carrying our sins. All those sins were resolved at the cross. All our sins were taken care of through Jesus' receiving the punishment for all those sins and the judgment for our sins completely ended there. God sees that cross and says to us, "Now you are righteous. You are holy. All your sins are washed away."

## Yes, I Am Righteous!

If we take the cross lightly and think only of the sins we committed, we can only say, "How can I say I am righteous? I am not righteous. I am dirty. I am filthy." But now we believe the promise of God.

"Ah, all my sins are washed away! Now I am righteous! I am clean!"

"That's right, God. I am righteous!"

Jacob could not believe it when God called him Israel.

"God, I am Jacob. I am not Israel. I am crooked and twisted. I deceived my older brother to steal his birthright, and again deceived my father saying that I was Esau to steal the blessing. And also to take Laban's sheep, I took rods of green poplar, hazel, and chestnut, and pilled white streaks to make spotted sheep. I committed these kinds of sins. This is how evil and dirty I am. God, I am Jacob, not Israel!"

Jacob could only say this. But God was different from Jacob.

"You are no longer Jacob, but Israel!"

According to the Word of God, from that day on, Jacob

became Israel.

The works of the Bible are the same. It was clearly water the servants at the wedding of the Cana of Galilee poured, but Jesus said, "Now it is not water anymore. It's wine." The water turned into wine through Jesus. Likewise, God changed us who are dirty.

"You are no longer a sinner. You are righteous!"

That is what God said.

*Being justified freely by his grace.* (Romans 3:24)

"Yes, God, I am righteous! I am sanctified!"

It is believing the Word of God. It is coming forth with the promise. The promise has nothing to do with my works. Becoming righteous is not because you have done something good, kind, or truthful. God, through His grace, has freely made us righteous.

In our eyes he is Jacob, but in God's eyes he is Israel. In our eyes it is water, but in Jesus' eyes it is wine. In our eyes we are sinners, but we are righteous in God's eyes. God's eyes are different from ours. Now do not believe in your eyes anymore but believe the eyes God sees through. When God calls you righteous, say, "I am righteous." When Jesus says that it is wine, say, "It is wine." When God says you are Israel, say, "I am Israel." Saying this and accepting it is true faith.

# 44

# *Have the Faith to Believe in the Promise*

*And Jacob lifted up his eyes, and looked, and, behold, Esau came, and with him four hundred men. And he divided the children unto Leah, and unto Rachel, and unto the two handmaids.* (Genesis 33:1)

## Now What Do I Do?

We are talking about how Jacob enters the land of Canaan from Padan-aram through the guidance of God. Jacob runs away to Padan-aram from Canaan in order to elude his older brother, Esau, then returns 20 years later. It has been 20 years and he was very curious as to how his brother's heart would be. 20 years earlier, Esau had tried to kill Jacob for stealing the birthright of the first-born and the blessing. "What will Esau think of me? Has his rage calmed down? What if he tries to kill me again?"

Because he had that heart, he first wanted to know his brother's heart and sent four servants to say, "Jacob is returning to meet you." But the servants returned and said, "We relayed your message, and your brother is on his way with 400 men." Upon hearing this, Jacob became afraid, thinking, "My older brother could have come alone, but coming with 400 men surely means that he is trying to kill me. He will destroy my entire family! I do have to see him, but now what do I do?"

Jacob agonized about this and then came up with a plan. He would first give many presents to Esau to melt his heart before he met him. He prepared sheep, cows, donkeys, and many others gifts to send before him. In case his brother would still be angry and attack, Jacob divided his household and cattle into two companies and thought, “One will escape if the other is smitten.” He did not group his children into one, but arrayed the maid-servants’ sons first, then others, then others, and made them to pass on.

## Useless Things That Arise from Distrust

Jacob has two methods with which to meet his brother Esau. One is his method and the other is the promise of God. When Jacob was going to Padan-aram from Canaan, God promised Jacob at Bethel, “Wherever you go I will be with you, protect you, watch over you, and will not leave you until you return to this land.” This promise remained in Jacob’s memory.

This story is interesting because, although Esau was bringing 400 men with him, God had made a promise to Jacob. God promised Jacob that He would protect and be with him until he returns to Canaan. If Jacob clearly believed in this promise, then God would protect him. What does it matter that Esau is bringing 400 men? What does it matter if Esau is bringing swords or bringing spears? If this were the case, Jacob would not have to use his human methods to prepare presents and to have one company escape when another is smitten. If God keeps the words of His promise, why would Jacob have to present gifts to Esau in order to melt his heart and think of escaping with one company? Because he ultimately did not believe that God would keep His promise that He would protect him, because he distrusted Him, he tried to protect his self. When do we need human methods? Human methods are evidence of faithlessness in God.

Jacob prepared gifts to present to Esau but his heart was not at peace. There was no guarantee that the gifts would melt Esau's heart to keep Jacob from death. He planned to escape with one company if another was smitten, but still he had no peace in his heart. How far could he run with children when there are 400 soldiers chasing after him? He had only chosen these methods because he had no other way.

Then Jacob finally met Esau.

*And Jacob lifted up his eyes, and looked, and behold, Esau came, and with him four hundred men. And he divided the children unto Leah, and unto Rachel, and unto the two hand maids.*

Jacob stood before his brother, Esau. And rather than bring swords or spears forward, Esau fell upon Jacob's neck and tearfully embraced him.

Ultimately, everything Jacob did was all in vain. That had all come from distrust. God promised that He would protect Jacob no matter what he does and because of that promise He was protecting Jacob and caring for him. Even when Laban was coming after Jacob, God told Laban, "Take heed that thou speak not to Jacob, either good or bad," and protected Jacob.

## From Another View . . .

This only seems like an ordinary story. However, in the world today, many people select these two paths Jacob had chosen in their spiritual lives. One is believing in the promise of God, and the other is doing it yourself because of unbelief in the promise of God. You being at work is not faith.

In the Bible, Saul was thrown away by God for giving an

offering to God. Why did he give the offering? God said He would protect him, but when he felt that that was not happening, he thought he should have God protect him and gave the offering. This offering is of distrust and thus, Saul was thrown away by God.

This is also true with our spiritual life. There are many things that happen because we do not have faith to believe in God, because of distrust. There are many people who especially agonize over coming before God because of sin. There are many who pray, "God, I am a sinner. Forgive my sins. I hope you will wash my sins away." The image of realizing their sins and asking for forgiveness appears truthful and beautiful, but from another view, they are praying for forgiveness because they are unable to believe that all of our sins have been forgiven through God sending Jesus to this earth and to the cross.

God did not just send Jesus to this earth to die on the cross just for the sake of Him dying on the cross. Jesus prayed to God before He hung on the cross.

"Father, if you will, I want to avoid this cup. But let it not be by my will, but through the will of the father."

Although Jesus was sincerely seeking, God did not have Jesus avoid the cross, but had Him bear it. Why was this so? It was because there is no other way to redeem our sins other than the cross. Therefore, the death of Jesus on the cross was not a vain death, but a death that washed all of our sins away as white as snow. If we believe this, we have to be free from sin. "I am free. It is true I sinned, but my sins are washed away. I am justified. I am holy."

Faith is going before God with this free heart. But people today do not have the faith to believe in God and therefore set up their own methods. They have the heart, "I will pray a little better, deeply realize my wrongfulness, and come before God with sorrow and agony. Then God will be pleased."

## When the Line of What You Do and What God Does Is Unclear

The story of Jacob shows the path of faith to us. Jacob had two ways before him that he could have taken. There was his method and there was the faith to believe in the promise of God. If Jacob believed the promise of God who said, "I am with you and will protect, care for, and never leave you no matter where you go," he would not have needed his own ways at all.

Likewise, if we have the clear faith that the blood Christ shed on the cross washed our sins away, there is nothing we have to do for sin. It is because Jesus already finished sin on the cross. But today, many people are unsure of their faith to believe in the crucifixion of Jesus washing their sins away. They thus pray, asking for forgiveness, and they try to do good themselves. They try to add their methods to this problem of having sins forgiven.

These methods are like the methods of Jacob to prepare gifts for Esau, and run away with one company when another is smitten. Jacob thinks that he is doing well, but all of these are from distrusting the promise. God promised to protect and to never leave Jacob no matter where he would go. What is the matter if Esau is bringing 400 men? What problem is it if 4,000 men were being brought, and what problems would there be if he were bringing 40,000 men?

"I am fine if God protects me! There is nothing to worry about!"

If Jacob believed this, why would he prepare gifts and why would he try to escape with one of his divided companies if the other was to be smitten? Ultimately, because of his distrust in the promise, Jacob had to prepare gifts for Esau, and set up the plan to escape with one company.

The problem is that our spiritual lives are this way. When we do not have faith in the fact that God is for us, we end up using our methods, our ways, and our means. Being faithful to your church, building chapels, and giving much offering may seem like great things, but they are nothing in the eyes of God. If our sins could be washed away with these things, or if these things could make us righteous, Jesus would not have been crucified. God knew that realizing our sins or acting with our zeal would not be good enough. Thus, He sent His son, Jesus, to be crucified. But we are unclear about this line. Because we are unclear about what we do and what God does, we think, "I should still do something," in our hearts. This is from distrust.

## If You Believe . . .

Loving folks, spiritual life is believing in God. It is believing in Jesus. How do you believe in God? How do you believe in Jesus? It is believing that Jesus washed all your sins away. If Jesus perfectly took care of all your sins on the cross, there is nothing you or I have to do for sins. Straining and laboring and sincerely praying to have your sins washed away may appear to be good and godly. But people do these things ultimately because they do not have faith that the blood of Jesus forgave their sins.

Yesterday, I called my wife as I was coming home from Daeduk Retreat Center.

"Honey, I left at 11 o'clock and I think I will be at home around 2 o'clock in the afternoon."

"Really? It's a little late, but I'll have lunch ready for you so come home quickly."

On our way home, we stopped at a service area. They sold lots of food there, but I did not have any although I was hungry. I had a cup of coffee with the brothers and said, "Let's go home. They have lunch prepared for us," and started heading home. Because of traffic, we arrived at home a little past two. My wife had prepared a delicious meal and we enjoyed it.

If I am unable to believe that my wife prepared lunch, I would say, "Let's get something to eat here," at the service area. However, because I clearly believe what my wife said, although I was a little hungry and although there was a lot of food there, I was able to hold off, go home, and eat. That is faith. Suppose my wife prepared all the food, but I say this upon coming home.

"Honey, I already ate."

"What? I prepared for you. . . ."

"I thought maybe you wouldn't prepare anything."

"No, I said I would prepare lunch for you."

"Yes, but how can I believe that?"

If this happened, how upset would my wife be?

When we read the Bible closely, this is exactly how our faith is. If the Bible says that God sent His son, Jesus Christ, to this earth and forgave our sins, then we have to believe that. If it says that Jesus washed our sins as white as snow on the cross, then we have to believe that. If it says that God does not remember our sins, we have to believe that. If we believe this, there is nothing we have to do for sins at all.

It is not that keeping the law or zealously serving God, itself, is bad. But because one cannot believe that God washed his sins away, he prays to have his sins washed and tries to take care of the problem of sin himself. This is wrong. These things appear to be truthful to you, but in the eyes of God, these things are from distrust. Saul sincerely gave the offering, but it was an offering he gave because he could not believe that God would protect him.

## I Believe that the Blood of Jesus Forgave This Sin Also

People believe in their own thoughts. They do not believe the Word of God. The main character of the 66 books of the Bible is Jesus Christ. It was prophesied that Christ would come to earth to deliver us from sin, and according to that promise, Jesus came to this earth in the body of a man. Then, according to the promise of God, He was crucified and forgave all of our sins.

Everyone, why do churches today have crosses perched on their buildings? It signifies the death of Jesus. It means that Jesus died for our sins. If Jesus died for our sins, then it is clear that our sins are washed away. If our sins are clearly and perfectly washed away, then there is nothing we have to do for sin. Jesus finished everything that needed to be done. But people ask for their sins to be washed away again because they do not believe that their sins have been washed away.

I am still lacking and weak. At times, I make mistakes and commit sins. However, I do not ask for my sins to be forgiven. I do not because it is so clearly recorded in the Bible that my sins are forgiven at the cross.

"God, I do not know why I am like this. I have these kinds of shortcomings, but I surely believe that even this sin was washed away through the blood of Jesus."

In the Old Testament, Israelites were stoned to death for disobeying the word, bitten to death by fiery serpents, killed by the earth swallowing them, burnt to death. . . . There are many stories of them being cursed. I was supposed to receive this kind of destruction, but Jesus died in my place on the cross. That death on the cross ended all the curse and destruction I was to receive, and ended all my sins. I clearly believe this. Thus, although I am lacking and weak, I come before God boldly with the faith that He is with me. Regardless of what I face, I have the faith, "This is not me going through this alone. God is with me. God helps me," and therefore, I can always boldly keep my heart toward God.

## Now Let Go of Everything You Are Doing

Once again, Jacob had two ways with which to meet Esau when Esau was bringing 400 men with him. One way was to believe in the promise of God, and the other was the human way; to try to melt Esau's heart. The second way is unnecessary if you have the faith to believe in God. He needed this second way because he did not have faith in God.

This is true with our spiritual lives as well. There are so many things we do because we do not have faith in Jesus. If you believe Jesus forgave your sins on the cross, there is nothing you have to do for sin. Everything already ended on the cross. However, people do not believe this truth.

Loving folks, at this very moment, leave everything you are doing behind and believe what Jesus has done. What Jesus has done is the most perfect. Believe that your sins are forgiven through the crucifixion of Jesus. Although in your thoughts it seems your sins are not forgiven and it feels like your sins remain, do not believe your thoughts but believe the words of the Bible. The Bible said, *I have blotted out . . . as a cloud thy sins: return unto me.* (Isaiah 44:22) It is telling us to return because our sins are all washed away. *But he was wounded for our transgressions, he was bruised for our iniquities.* (Isaiah 53:5)

I hope you will believe that the death of Jesus, the sacrifice for us, did not half-heartedly take care of our sins, but has perfectly made them as white as snow.

From time to time, you may feel guilty or have problems with sin in your heart, but you should say, "It is true I have sinned, I am dirty and evil, but this sin is also washed because Jesus died for all of these sins. I am clean," and come to God boldly by faith. If you are not this way, but feel bold when you do well and do not feel bold when you do wrong, that is not faith. The Bible is teaching us this truth through Jacob. I hope you will all have the faith to believe in God's promise.

# 45

## *Go Up to Bethel*

*And Dinah, the daughter of Leah, which she bare unto Jacob, went out to see the daughters of the land. And when Shechem the son of Hamor the Hivite, prince of the country, saw her, he took her, and lay with her, and defiled her* (Genesis 34:1-2)

## We May Know the Road's Exact Width

I have a younger cousin who lives in Hiroshima, Japan. He used to be a race car driver. Now that he is older and retired, he now works as a civil engineer. He makes bridges, tunnels, and roads in his city. I once visited his house and he told me, "Cousin, I built this bridge. I build this road. I built this tunnel." Roads in Hiroshima are very rugged with many rocks. He said that he had built most of the roads in the area. We talked about many things in the car, and I asked him, "Hey, it seems that it was terribly difficult to dig these tunnels. Wasn't it hard?" He answered that it was not hard at all. I then asked if there were anything that was hard and he told me that in Japan receiving the completion approval for the road was the most difficult. He told me that even a one centimeter error in the width of the road is unacceptable.

The roads in Japan are very straight and clean, and I thought, "This is so because of the inspectors." If a person who builds roads thinks, "This is probably good enough," he will be in big trouble. Unless he follows the standards, he has to fix all that he has already built. My cousin told me about how extremely difficult that was. The world we see with our eyes can easily be understood this way. We can easily tell whether a road is one centimeter too wide or too narrow by simply inspecting it. However, it is difficult to pinpoint such things in the world of the heart. As a result, many people in spiritual life think, "If I do this much it means I have good faith in God. I am better than Deacon Kim. I diligently gave tithes and attended early morning services amidst difficulties. If I am doing this much it means my spiritual life is going well."

## Why Is He Having Me Suffer Such Hardship?

All of a sudden, a terrible problem arises in Jacob's life in Genesis chapter 34. His daughter was raped and taken captive by the son of the chief of that area while she was out enjoying herself. They had too many men for Jacob to fight them and he was at a loss of what to do. When we read of this in the Bible we think, "Jacob believes in God. Why is God allowing Jacob to suffer this kind of hardship?" Jacob's loving daughter being raped by the son of the chief of the Shechem tribe tore Jacob's heart apart and made him bitter.

But when we read the Bible, we can feel that Jacob's thoughts were different from God's. For 20 years Jacob herded his uncle, Laban's, flock in Padan-aram and was very tired and exhausted. He then left Padan-aram without his uncle's knowledge to return to the land of Canaan, but Laban later found out and pursued Jacob. However, God appeared to Laban in a dream telling him to not speak good or evil to Jacob, and Laban went away without striking Jacob. Afterwards, Jacob's older brother, Esau, brought 400 men with him when Jacob was near Canaan. Jacob was greatly afraid, but he was very happy when his brother treated him kindly. Jacob had to go to Canaan after Esau departed from him, but when he arrived at the land of Succoth, Jacob had the heart to remain there because the land was vast and good.

*And Jacob came to Shalem, a city of Shechem, which is in the land of Canaan, when he came from Padan-aram; and pitched his tent before the city. And he bought a parcel of a field, where he had spread his tent, at the hand of the children of Hamor, Shechem's father, for an hundred pieces of money. And he erected there an altar, and called it El-Elohe-Israel.* (Genesis 33:18-20)

Jacob arrived at Succoth and thought, "It would be nice to stay here. Can't I just call God and erect an altar here?" However, God was not pleased with Jacob staying there. Thus, his daughter, Dinah, was violated. A war broke out over this, and when Jacob fell into difficulty, he heard the voice of God telling him, "Go up to Bethel."

The will of God was for Jacob to go to Bethel, but Jacob just remained in Succoth. It was not that Jacob sinned, did terrible things, or lived riotously in Succoth, he just built an altar there and sought God saying, "El-Elohe-Israel. (God is the God of Israel)" But why did God allow Jacob's daughter to be raped?

One thing we have to remember is that just because one is going astray from the will of God does not mean he is sinning only and doing wicked things. God did not want Jacob to remain in Succoth, but to go up to Bethel. But Jacob thought, "I can just call God here. I built an altar here and I am praying," and simply remained in Succoth.

## Upon Reflecting on My Life

In my spiritual life, I once had time to look back and reflect upon my past. When I looked back, I saw that there were many failures in things for which I had thought, "If I do this, this will go well." When I was planning such things, they seemed that they would go well because I cannot see the future. However, when I actually clashed against these things, I often ended up in failure. On the other hand, I saw that the things that I thought to be difficult and impossible were accomplished beautifully when I relied and looked only to God. Afterwards, even though I thought my ways to be good, I felt, "Before, I thought this would work out, but it didn't . . . ," and I lost the heart to trust myself. Evil and dirty hearts always sprang up in me, and because my heart is dishonest, deceitful, and lustful, I one day came to discover that I should not follow the thoughts that arise from within. Before this, I was not actually believing in God, but believing in myself. I followed my thoughts in everything I did. I only followed the words of God that I liked in my heart and did not follow the words I disliked. In reality, I was not believing in God, but believing in myself.

However, looking back upon my life, the heart to trust myself came crumbling down. "I should not trust myself! I cannot follow my thoughts!" After I came to fully realize that I should not follow my thoughts, I could no longer trust myself. No matter how good a thought seemed to me, I could say, "If I continue this way I will fail! This will ruin me!" and draw a clear line in my heart and keep to it.

I had many difficulties in my life. I quietly looked back

upon those difficulties. If a sheep were on the right path, why would its shepherd keep tapping it with a stick to keep it from going astray? The shepherd does so because the sheep is trying to go astray. He hits it with the stick to make it stay with the flock. I thought, "Why would God give me those hardships even though He loves me? Why would He give me those problems?" Right then I came to realize how I lived with a heart different form God's, a heart that said, "This is enough for God to be pleased." I thought, "I pray hard, witness, and read the Bible, shouldn't that be enough?" But God did not think so. Therefore, God gave me many difficulties.

Upon knowing this, I came to distrust my thoughts and myself and came to have the faith to believe in God. When I threw my thoughts away and believed the Word of God, amazingly, God began to open my eyes towards the Word of God. The Bible said, "It is more blessed to give than to receive," but I did not believe those words. I thought the words, "Those who will be exalted will be abased and the abased shall be exalted," were fine words, but I did not believe them in my heart. I liked receiving; I liked being exalted. However, upon knowing that my thoughts were wrong and as I denied myself, the faith to believe in God began to arise inside me. From then on, God began to work within me. Afterwards, my life became extremely blessed.

## Evil Have the Days of the Years of My Life Been

When Jacob stood before Pharaoh the king of Egypt, Pharaoh asked, "Hold old art thou?"

Right then Jacob answered like this:

"I am one hundred thirty. I have not attained unto the days of the years of the life of my fathers, but evil have the days of the years of my life been."

Jacob was craftier than anyone else. He stole the birthright and the blessing from his older brother, Esau. Nevertheless, even when we carefully look into this, God already told Rebekah, while Jacob and Esau were in her womb, that, "Two nations shall come from thee. One nation will be stronger than the other, and the elder shall serve the younger." God had blessed Jacob, but Jacob tried to gain the blessings of God through his own methods. Therefore, he ran away to Padan-aram when his brother tried to kill him. Jacob loved Rachel while he was at Padan-aram. He served for seven years for Rachel at his uncle's house, but he ended up marrying Leah. God continually interfered with whatever Jacob was doing to have him throw away human methods.

People do not like to follow when it seems that goals will not be accomplished even if it is the will of God. We all have that kind of a heart. That is not spiritual life. When my cousin was building roads, even though he wanted to build according to his own will, he had to construct completely according to the blue prints. It does not matter how well the roads or bridges are built. If they are different from the blue prints, they will not be approved. Why wouldn't my cousin think, "I should build the bridge here like this?" But since he knows exactly that no matter how well the roads are made and how well the bridges are built, they are useless if they are not approved. Therefore, he throws his thoughts away and builds roads, constructs bridges, and digs tunnels according to the blue prints.

Spiritual life is exactly the same. If you do not have a certain thought, then you will simply receive the word exactly as it is. Then spiritual life is very easy. However, Satan continually gives you the heart that you should not believe the word as it is and makes you feel as if your thoughts are right. You must believe the Word of God in spiritual life, but your thoughts constantly arise to make you feel as though things will not work out and you will be ruined if you do according to the Word of God. It seems as though your thoughts are more right and better than the Word of God. Therefore, many people continuously pursue after their ways and their thoughts. If they continue forward this way, they ultimately arrive at difficulty and failure because those ways differ from the will of God.

## Go Up to Bethel

God told Jacob to, "Go up to Bethel (the house of God)." Before, Jacob could not hear the voice of God and could not see Bethel. He simply thought, "Succoth is pretty good. It would be good to build an altar and give service to God here. God did not want this, however. What did the tribe of Shechem want when Dinah, Jacob's daughter, was raped? They proposed, "Let us marry one another. Would it not be good if your sons could marry our daughters and if our daughters marry your sons?" Because Christ had to be born among the descendants of Israel, God did not want the children of Israel to become of mixed blood with other tribes. That was why He blocked it. When Jacob was cornered and had no more ways of his own, he finally heard the voice of God. "Go up to Bethel."

Jacob then went up to Bethel.

Our spiritual life is exactly the same as this. There are many who say that they believe in the Word of God, yet they trust in their own thoughts. It is not a problem when the Word of God is the same as your thoughts, but when the Word of God differs from your thoughts, you have extreme difficulties following the Word of God. And you suffer as you do so. Then you ultimately select your own methods and your own ways. Even so, you think that God will be pleased with you because you are seeking God like Jacob. This is what God blocks.

## What Is Right, Good, and Beautiful?

I attended a Presbyterian church before receiving salvation. At that time, I suffered much because of sin and I labored not to sin. I tried not to lie or hate others. I would become determined, resolved, and I prayed much as well.

"God, I committed this and this kind of sin. Do not allow me to sin at all today."

I prayed sincerely. Nevertheless, I would sin again every day. I thought, "Why doesn't God help me? I hate sinning, but why does He leave me to sin?" Right then, I did not know that I was wrong in front of God. Me trying not to sin and coming before Him through not sinning, by trying to pray, giving offering and bringing these to God, I came to know that all of these were wrong. After time passed and upon me having faith, I came to know how foolish all those things were.

Doing good deeds may seem good to some people, but in the eyes of God they are like filthy rags. One day I was reading the Bible and Isaiah chapter 64 said, *all our righteousnesses are as filthy rags.* I thought doing good and living truthfully were all righteous things, but in the eyes of God they were like filthy rags. In the eyes of God, our righteousness, our good, all of these things are like filthy rags. Then what is right, good, and beautiful in the eyes of God? The righteousness of Jesus Christ and only that is true righteousness.

God told us to come to Bethel. Jacob built an altar in Succoth and called the name of God, but God allowed Dinah to be raped so that Jacob could not remain in Succoth. When we ask, "God, can't I just pray hard? Isn't keeping the law enough? Isn't serving God with all my heart enough?" God answers that they are not. It means we cannot stand before God with things that come from us.

God, in many places in the book of Romans, says that because we are all dirty and evil, we cannot come before God with the righteousness we have. However, because we continually try to come before God with our own righteousness, God has us sin to break down our righteousness. God breaks the heart, "If I do this, I will be good and righteous. I will come before God." Because your righteousness will not do, God has you come forth with the righteousness of Jesus, the goodness of Jesus, and the holiness of Jesus. That is Bethel, the house of God.

## We Must Depart Succoth and Go to Bethel

God wanted to lead Jacob to Bethel, but Jacob wanted to remain in Succoth. God leads us the same way He loved Jacob. We think that our goodness, our helping orphans, our helping the poor, and our giving offering without others' knowledge is precious. But God says that they are hypocritical. Why? It is because everything that man does comes from an evil heart. God accepts people who come forth with what Jesus accomplished on the cross, not our righteousness, our good, or what we have done. He wants us to accept the righteousness Jesus accomplished and then come to Him.

Succoth shows your good, your effort, and your well-doing, while Bethel represents what Jesus has accomplished. God wants us to quickly depart from our doing well and good and tells us to go to Bethel. Just as Jacob remained at Succoth, there are many people who try to come before God with their good, their righteousness, and with what they have done well. However, we must leave that place and go to Bethel. We should not labor to wash our sins, but look to Jesus washing our sins. We should not exalt our righteousness, but exalt the righteousness of Jesus. When you throw all of your good away and go forward with the righteousness of Jesus, God will be satisfied and pleased.

# 46

# *If You Hear the Voice of God*

*And God said unto Jacob, Arise, go up to Bethel, and dwell there: and make there an altar unto God, that appeared unto thee when thou fleddest from the face of Esau thy brother. Then Jacob said unto his household, and to all that were with him, Put away the strange gods that are among you, and be clean, and change your garments: And let us arise, and go up to Bethel; and I will make there an altar unto God, who answered me in the day of my distress, and was with me in the way which I went.* (Genesis 35:1-3)

## Because You Are in God's Net

When we precisely know the will of God and stand on His path, everything becomes very easy from that point on. From time to time I hear people say, "Spiritual life is difficult, tiring, and miserable." Spiritual life is difficult because your thoughts collide against the Word of God. If you know that your thoughts are useless before the Word of God, no matter how good your thoughts seem to be, spiritual life is so easy.

As we learned in the last sermon, God wanted Jacob to go to Bethel but Jacob wanted to remain at Succoth and built an altar there. If things were to go well, Jacob would have continued to remain in Succoth; thus, God had to give Jacob a hardship.

This is what people say.

"God, He's the God of love. He is for us and loves us. Why is He allowing this kind of hardship to befall us? Why is God allowing me to go through this kind of tribulation if He exists? Where is God? I lived so honestly, but why do I have to go through this?"

If we objectively think about this, we see that people think that they are walking God's path because they read the Bible and give offering, regardless of the fact that they live following their own thoughts without knowing the precise will of God. How could that path be the same as God's when they do not have ears to hear the voice of God and do not know the deep heart of God? That is why God leads us.

What happens when a fish is caught in a net while it is swimming in the sea? It becomes entangled. "What did I just run into?" It turns around and swims and it is okay. Then again while it is swimming around, it runs into something. Then the space becomes smaller and smaller, and eventually it is captured. God puts us into His net and leads us into His world. That is why we run into things as we go on to do something. When we turn around from the frustration, it seems for a little while that things are okay, but we crash into something again. It is because we are in God's net. Our lives become much better when we fully understand this.

## Through Discovering the Secrets of the Gospel from the Scriptures

I quietly thought one day after receiving salvation, "What can I do to please God?" God forgave all the sins of man through the blood of His son, Jesus. However, as I saw that many people were inside sin because they could not realize this, I had the heart, "God would want me to allow these people to realize that their sins are forgiven. God would be pleased with me preaching the gospel." When I had assurance that God would be pleased with my preaching the gospel, I did so from that day on. I did not know how to preach the gospel well. However, I wanted to preach the gospel. As I stayed in a small village in the mountains of a town called Apgok-dong, God taught me, as I read the Bible, how to preach the gospel.

I once read the Pentatude of Moses. I was reading Genesis, Exodus, Leviticus, Numbers, and Deuteronomy, and the Scriptures I once thought to be difficult were so much fun. The secrets of redemption were so vividly hidden in the words of Moses' Pentatude. When I read Genesis, I read about the aprons of fig leaves and the coats of skins in chapter 3. "Ah! Just like the aprons of fig leaves, my actions may hide my blemishes, but the redemption through Jesus at the cross can cover my blemishes perfectly like the coats of skin!" I was able to clearly see such things.

I read Exodus. The second half of Exodus talks about the tabernacle, and it is complicated, talking about the width being so and so cubits, the length being so and so cubits, and the height being so and so cubits. I then read about the mercy seat.

"What is a mercy seat?"

"Ah, it's the place where sins are forgiven."

"They call the top part of the ark the mercy seat. I wonder why they call that the mercy seat."

I was very curious. When I read further through the Bible, I saw that blood was sprinkled upon the mercy seat when sin offerings were given.

"Ah, this is where the blood is sprinkled. Since the blood is sprinkled here, the mercy seat becomes the place where sin is redeemed! Wherever the blood of Jesus is sprinkled is the mercy seat!"

As I realized this, I thought in my heart, "Sin is redeemed anywhere the blood of Jesus is sprinkled. I should tell people that Jesus shed His blood on the cross for our sins. If they accept this; if the blood of Jesus is sprinkled on their heart, they will be redeemed."

I read Leviticus. Chapter 4 talked about the sin offering. It also talked about the sin offering for a congregation. I thought about this.

"The whole congregation of Israel sinned. Therefore, the priest presents the sin offering. . . ."

When I thought about this, I could feel that there must have been many people in the congregation of Israel that did not know the priest was presenting the sin offering. There were 600,000 adult males, so how could all these people know? When a priest would present a sin offering for the congregation, there must have been people who were taking naps, out for a drink, taking a bath, or working. They did not know that the priest was presenting a sin offering for them, but their sins were forgiven when the priest presented the sin offering.

"That's right! I didn't know when Jesus was being crucified, but my sins were all washed away then!"

I read Numbers. In Numbers chapter 21, those who were bitten by the fiery serpents looked to the brass serpent and were healed. But in John chapter 3 Jesus said, "And as Moses lifted up the serpent in the wilderness, even so must the Son of man be lifted up."

"If that's so, the brass serpent represents Jesus!"

"Then why do those who were bitten by the fiery serpent live when they look at the brass serpent?"

"Ah, when I, who am bitten by sin, look to the cross, my sins are forgiven at the cross!"

It was very comfortable preaching the gospel as I came to know these things, one by one.

## In Any Wise Let the Dam Go

I read Deuteronomy. In chapter 22, it says, *If a bird's nest chance to be before thee in the way in any tree, or on the ground, whether they be young ones, or eggs, and the dam sitting upon the young, or upon the eggs, thou shalt not take the dam with the young: But thou shalt in any wise let the dam go, and take the young to thee.*

"Why is God saying that the dam that sits on the young or the eggs should be released?"

Not just any mother bird, but when a dam is sitting on its young, what does this represent? Sitting on eggs is to gain new life, and sitting on the young also represents caring for the young.

"Ah, I am the dam! I, leading people who are not born again to become born again, am sitting on the eggs. And preaching the word to born again brothers and sisters is caring for the young. I, who am preaching the gospel, am this dam!"

As I read these words, I thought, "This bird may get caught by someone, but God is telling this person to release it. If I preach the gospel for people to become born again and if I preach the word for young brothers and sisters to grow, plagues will not be able to hurt me even if I run into them!" I had hope and strength.

I lived very busily preaching the gospel. From last year, friends of mine saw me in the newspapers or on television and started contacting me, and I have been meeting these friends from my hometown. I was so happy to see these friends from childhood at my age of much past sixty. However, I was so shocked to hear about how they had lived as we talked about our lives. My friends became entangled in plagues in their lives. One friend failed in business and agonized about it so much that he became mentally weak. Another friend suffered from sicknesses and lost all of his energy trying to be healed. One friend of mine became bankrupt and was on the run from the police. It was so bad that he could not go to his daughter's wedding and wept as he looked at his daughter's wedding from the roof of a building across the street. When I listened to this from them, it felt as though I was living in a different world. My friends were in hardship and their faces seemed very bent. I was different from my friends because, although many plagues and hardships came to me, each time the Lord had me avoid them.

When my heart was in a terrible condition and had no way of getting fixed, God healed it completely. When my stomach was terribly bad, God healed it. He fixed my ear when it was ill. . . . I, too, had many plagues, miseries, difficult circumstances, but God told them to release me, for it was by the Word of God that such plagues could not capture me. They tried to hold me, but released me. This life of being released from plagues, being blessed, and receiving grace is such an amazing life.

## After the Word Enters the Heart

I did not know how to preach the gospel, but God made me realize, "Ah, this is how I should preach the gospel." When I explained to people in detail the gospel of forgiveness of sins, I discovered that people would listen to the Word and say, "My sins are forgiven! I am now righteous!" and believe that their sins were forgiven. Among them, there were many who really wanted to know if their sins were forgiven but could not. They had thus tried to experience speaking in tongues, feeling something burning in their hearts, or other such supernatural things to gain confirmation that their sins were forgiven. I have never spoken in tongues. I have fasted for a few days, but I could never even imagine fasting and praying for 40 days. I have absolutely no confidence that I could do such a thing. I also have never directly heard the voice of God or seen visions. I just read the words of the Bible and simply believed them to be the words of God.

While reading Deuteronomy again, I read, *Thou shalt not muzzle the ox when he treadeth out the corn.* (Deuteronomy 25:4) I liked this so much. It was saying to not muzzle the ox that walks on the corn or treads the corn, meaning let it eat freely.

"Ah, God will not block my mouth which is preaching the gospel to lead people to the Lord. He will not have me go hungry."

The Scriptures, one by one, came upon my heart as hope and faith. I had no idea how I should deal with people or how to lead the church, but the Scriptures taught me about all of these things as I read the Bible.

Before, I had disinclined my ears to the Word of God because I was arrogant. I simply ran forward however I thought and worked. Nothing ever went properly when I did this. However, after the Word of God entered my heart, even if things did not go well, I could be assured, "This will work because this is the promise of God."

I preach the gospel of the forgiveness of sins to people. When we read the Bible, we see that it is filled with the words of the forgiveness of sins. When I speak to some people about the forgiveness of sins from Genesis, they receive the forgiveness of sins and rejoice. However, some say that they are not able to understand. Then I speak to them of the gospel from Exodus. If this does not work, I speak from Leviticus, and if this still does not work then I speak from Romans, then Hebrews. . . . Then people receive salvation one by one. They receive salvation because they do not believe their thoughts but believe the Word of God which clearly records that our sins are washed away. I am so thankful. Then they change. They seek the word, preach the gospel. . . . It is so wonderful. We then gather every evening to share testimonies and the word and we are so joyful.

## Story of Two People

My life, after getting married, was very difficult. We once ran out of food and my wife and I went to an orphanage. We said to the orphanage director, "We are people who preach the gospel to children and we want to plant the heart of God in the children here. If you would give us the opportunity to, we will teach the Bible to the children for an entire week for free." The director gave us permission to do so. We then preached the gospel to the orphans there. When it was lunch time, they gave us food. We ate so thankfully. We preached the gospel in the afternoon, had dinner, and preached the gospel in the evening as well. It became night and we were on our way home. It was a two and a half mile walk, but it did not feel tiring, but rather we felt extremely happy.

A few years later, we held Bible studies at the currency press in Gyeongsan. I went there every Thursday, and I so enjoyed the two mile walk I would take after the Bible study through the dark woods behind Youngnam University. Thinking, "Okhee got saved today! Soyoung will be the next one to be saved!" I saw the stars sparkling in the dark night alone as I walked, and it filled me with happiness.

I am so happy that I can preach the word at the podium; I am so joyful to be reading the Bible; and I am so peaceful that I can pray. All of these things are not through me, but it is Jesus Christ leading me this way. I had not known this kind of a world before and for a very long time I lived in my thoughts, in my plans, and in the faith to believe myself. I had no idea how things could go well and tried to use my own intelligence and methods, but after some time, they all ended in failure.

The book of Luke always talks about two kinds of people. There is Jesus who came wearing the body of man, and there is man. On the surface, they are both human, but everything Jesus did succeeded. However, everything that man did without Jesus, with his own wisdom and his own ways, all ended in failure.

Luke chapter 10 talks about a certain man going down from Jerusalem to Jericho, falling among thieves, and failing. He had plans to make money, buy a good house, get married, and live happily, but God was missing from his plans. Chapter 15 talks about the younger son taking the great wealth he received from the father, going to a far away country, and failing. He never thought this would happen to him if he leaves the father's house and goes to a far away country. But things did not go according to his heart, but failed. Chapter 16 talks about how the rich man wearing coats of fine purple linen fared sumptuously every day. It seemed that he succeeded in his life, but we see him dying and suffering in hell. Ultimately, his life was a failure.

The image of man seen in the book of Luke is a complete failure. There is one clear result. "Everything I do is a failure. Everything Jesus does is a success." When this result is clear, from then on, you can no longer live following your thoughts or methods. It is not that I am spiritually keen that I am led by the Holy Spirit. However, because I came to know clearly that my methods will not do, I was able to incline my ears to the Lord, look to God, and go forth relying on Him.

## If You Hear the Voice of God

Jacob heard the voice of God he had not heard before. In chapter 33, Jacob builds booths and an altar at Succoth and he seeks God. In chapter 35, when he realized that what he did was a failure, God spoke to Jacob. People without faith do not try to hear the voice of God, but only speak their thoughts to God. However, people who listen to the voice of God do not make only their own prayers, but open the Bible and hear the voice of God.

As I read the Pentatude of Moses, read Judges, read First and Second Samuel, discovered God, and heard the voice of God, I saw how foolish and stupid I had lived.

Loving folks, spiritual life is believing in God. To have faith, we have to first realize that our methods are wrong. When you become freed from your ways, you are able to have the faith to believe in God. Right then God works with power inside of us. Regardless of how your thoughts have been until now, empty all of those thoughts and listen to the word God speaks to you. Incline your ears to the voice of God. If you hear the voice of God, it is no longer the path you go. It is the path God takes. Through hearing the voice of God, Noah started to build the ark, Abraham gained a son, and Moses went before Pharaoh. They were not paths of their own, but paths God showed them. I hope that you will not take your own paths, but walk the path of God.

# 47

# *From Benoni to Benjamin*

*And they journeyed from Bethel; and there was but a little way to come to Ephrath: and Rachel travailed, and she had hard labour. And it came to pass, when she was in hard labour, that the midwife said unto her, Fear not; thou shalt have this son also. And it came to pass, as her soul was in departing, (for she died) that she called his name Benoni: but his father called him Benjamin.* (Genesis 35:16-18)

## Rachel's Life Versus Leah's Life

Rachel was a woman with a beautiful face. One look at her could attract any man. Because she lacked nothing, she could always be bold and confident. On the other hand, Leah lacked much and had nothing but shame. She always lived feeling small. From a human perspective Rachel excelled in everything while Leah was lacking. But this made it difficult for Rachel to become close to God, but it allowed Leah to come close to God.

During Jesus' time, people such as scribes, Pharisees, and priests were people who were good from a human perspective. On the contrary, people like the publican, the woman taken in adultery, or harlots were dirty, useless people. The important thing is that the scribes and Pharisees may be better and more righteous than the publicans or harlots, but they cannot stand before God with that.

Many people today have their standards of spiritual life set upon man rather than God because they are unable to meet God. People think, "My spiritual life is better than his," and assume that their spiritual lives are great. However, God said that all of man's righteousness must crumble down because there is wickedness inside of man. Therefore, human goodness does not help in having faith, but rather deters it. Apostle Paul said that He considered everything he knew to be a loss. He knew knowledge and experience to be good things in the past, but now he saw that those things were distractions keeping him from relying on God.

Rachel and Leah lived together with their husband Jacob. Because Jacob loved Rachel, Rachel lacked nothing. However, she could not have a child. Thus, she threw a fit telling her husband to give her a son and used human methods to try to gain a son through her hand maid. There was nothing Leah could hope for herself, thus she relied on God. In the end, ugly Leah had many sons, while the beautiful Rachel ended her life in darkness.

## Not the Son of Sadness but the Son of the Right Hand

Today I will talk about Rachel's death. Rachel wanted a child very badly. She finally had one, and named him Joseph. "Joseph" means, "The Lord shall add to me another son." Afterwards, Rachel had her second child. How happy she must have been! However, she went into labor as Jacob's family was moving and was traveling along rough roads. When a woman is badly bleeding in her labor, she will in most cases die if the doctor is unable to control the bleeding. There were no doctors with this knowledge in Rachel's time and perhaps that was why her bleeding could not be stopped, and she was dying.

Fortunately, she gave birth and it was a son. Her midwife said, "Don't worry. It's another son." That was how she had a son, and she should have been very happy. But Rachel began to think.

"I did have a son, but I am dying now. How sad he will be without his mother! How painful it will be!"

When she thought of her son's future, it was so miserable so she named her son "Benoni (son of sadness)" and passed away.

Jacob saw all of this taking place. Rachel trusted herself so she thought it would be the end with her death. However, in Jacob's heart was God. God promised Abraham, Isaac, and Jacob that He would give them many children like the stars in the sky and the sands of the sea. Therefore, this son was also part of the process of this promise becoming fulfilled.

"If so, then how is he a son of sadness? There are times of sadness and pain in life, but this child is not Benoni."

Jacob changed the child's name to "Benjamin (the son of the right hand)." From then on the son of sadness changed into the "son of the right hand."

Had the name of the son of sadness remained as Rachel had given, that child would have always carried that title of sadness in his name.

"Son of sadness, come and eat."

"Son of sadness, let's go play."

"Son of sadness, let's sing a song."

In the eyes of Rachel, it was true that he is the son of sadness. His mother died through his birth, he cannot be breastfed without his mother, and so how will he grow? But from another perspective, why is he the son of sadness when God is with him?

Let's think about Joseph's case. Joseph was hated by his brothers, was sold, and became a servant to Potiphar, the Egyptian. He could very well say, "I am miserable!" Afterwards he was framed by Potiphar's wife and went to prison. "Why? Why is this happening to me? This is so painful and I feel miserable!" He may very well say this. However, God was with his life and he had another view that said, "This is not sadness. This is a prelude to a blessing."

## Another Eye

People of faith do not only look through their own eyes. Our view is crooked because it was formed through our ancestors Adam and Eve eating the fruit of the knowledge of good and evil. Even if we clearly see and confirm through our own eyes, it is completely different from seeing through the eyes of God. Therefore, it does not mean that just because you have clearly seen and known it that it is accurate. But there are many people who with eyes different from God's boast aloud that what they have seen is right.

When I read the Bible, God's eyes were completely different from mine. When the son of God, Jesus, went to the wedding at Cana of Galilee and they were in need of wine, He told the servants of the house to fill some waterpots with water, and they did so. It was water in the eyes of the servants, but it was wine in Jesus' eyes. The eyes of Jesus and the eyes of the servants differed while looking at the same thing. Whose eyes are right? Lazarus died. Facing these circumstances, the eyes Martha and Mary saw through completely differed from those of Jesus. Martha said, "Lazarus is dead. He is rotting and stinking." Jesus said, "No. Your brother will live." That is how the whole Bible goes. When God told Abraham that He would give him a son, Abraham thought, "How can a one hundred-year-old man have a son? Sarah is ninety nine. . . . This is impossible."

But God said, "Your wife Sarah will bear you a son."

## When We See a New World

As we have lived in this world, Satan has planted distrust in us. As we were deceived many times by people around us, we have lived believing only in ourselves. We believe our experience, our knowledge, and believe what we have seen. We think whatever fits those things are accurate. However, this is different from the viewpoint of God.

We established alternative schools within our mission. I went to the opening of one of them to preach the word. Forty students were starting school there and they were deviant students who could not adapt to regular schools. Some of them had long, dyed hair, and none of them looked like students. The students were so ashamed they had their heads down. Most of them smoked and some female students were even pregnant, and didn't even know it at the time. I thought, "Why do these students live like this?" I felt that they lived like this because they wanted to live this way. I told Pastor Wook Yong Kim, the principal, "Leave the students as they are and show them something better than what they have now. Show them something brighter in Jesus."

Afterwards, there were many problems. Once, some students ran away, stole a woman's purse, were arrested, and put in jail. The principal had to go there and beg to get them out. That was how the time passed. About 10% of them left the school, but all those who remained changed. These students saw a new world. Before attending this school, they liked the life without discretion so they lived without wanting to throw it away. That was how in darkness they lived, but as they saw a new world, their hearts changed.

It is difficult for us to try to change ourselves because we try while trusting our own thoughts. The eyes we see through must be changed. We must distrust what we see, hear, and experience. We must trust Jesus. In my eyes I cannot walk when I am a paralytic, but I can walk if Jesus tells me to walk. In my eyes, someone may be a leper, but he is clean if Jesus says he is. In my eyes it is water, but it is wine if Jesus calls it wine. That is not believing in yourself but in Jesus.

People believe themselves rather than Jesus. Because people believe in their own experience, knowledge, and methods, they do not follow the Word of God when it does not fit their heart and when it seems that a loss will come about. That is why God becomes small and powerless in their lives. When we accept Jesus in our hearts as savior, as Lord, when Jesus is higher than our thoughts God begins to work in our lives. He works when we accept through faith into our heart the fact that Jesus' thoughts are right rather than how I see things to be. When God works, amazing things we could never have imagined start to be accomplished.

Many people today live having fallen into the pit of believing in themselves. Because they have been deceived so much by the people around them, they trust no one and try to only trust themselves. The more hardhearted a person's heart becomes, the more he is unable to trust others. Drug addicts never listen to anyone. The mentally ill have weak hearts and do not listen to others, but only exert their own words. People who have enough space in their heart have the heart to listen and understand the words of people with opinions different from their own. But people who have shallow and hardened hearts continually exert only themselves.

## Look to the Heart of Jesus

Clearly this was a son of sadness to Rachel. But he, like the name Jacob had given him, became Benjamin (the son of the right hand) and served as the son of the right hand to free his brothers when they were captured by Joseph.

Faith is not trusting yourself, but Jesus. God said, "My thoughts are different from your thoughts." If you trust yourself, you are living your life. People who trust God do not live their lives but God's life. If you live the life of yourself, it seems that your goodness and your efforts to live righteously will go well, but not long afterwards all those things fail and end in emptiness. You may try tithing and keeping the Ten Commandments to establish yourself. If you truly try these things, you will realize how vain this is. Then you become able to follow the Lord's thoughts rather than your own.

A lady was making kimchi, and her mother-in-law came to her and said, "Honey, don't do it like that. Try it like this," and taught her how to make it. The daughter-in-law wanted to do it her own way, but when she followed her mother-in-law's advice, the kimchi was indeed very delicious. From then on, the daughter-in-law's methods began to resemble the methods of the mother-in-law. We should also not just live with our methods, but for once look to Jesus' heart. Surely Benjamin was a son of sadness in Rachel's eyes, but he was the son of the right hand in the eyes of Jacob. The circumstances were pain, sadness, and suffering when Paul was locked in prison at Philippi. However, Paul had new eyes and thus praised and thanked God. Then that place changed into a glittering place of glory.

## Receiving the Forgiveness of Sins

This is also true with you receiving the forgiveness of sins. It is not that you have to check with your eyes that your sins have been forgiven. It is not that you have to feel that your sins are forgiven in your heart. You have to see whether your sins were forgiven or not from God's eyes. Suppose you were a filthy, dirty sinner with many flaws. Then, open the Bible to see, "How is it in God's eyes?" Isaiah chapter 53 records:

*But he was wounded for our transgressions, he was bruised for our iniquities: the chastisement of our peace was upon him; and with his stripes we are healed. All we like sheep have gone astray; we have turned every one to his own way; and the LORD hath laid on him the iniquity of us all.* (Isaiah 53:5-6)

God says that He has laid all our sins upon Jesus. God says this in Hebrews chapter 10, verse 17.

*And their sins and iniquities will I remember no more.*

Isaiah chapter 44, verse 22 records:

*I have blotted out, as a thick cloud, thy transgressions, and as a cloud, thy sins: return unto me; for I have redeemed thee.*

Romans chapter 3, verses 23 through 24 record:

*For all have sinned, and come short of the glory of God; Being justified freely by his grace, through the redemption that is in Christ Jesus:*

Rachel named her son as she died, "You are Benoni," meaning the son of sadness. But Jacob changed his name to Benjamin, saying, "No, you are the son of the right hand." Was he the son of sadness? No. According to Jacob's faith, he became the son of the right hand.

In our eyes it is true that we are sinners. We have sinned, committed evil, and have lived filthy, lustful, deceitful lives. We have also sinned every day. But how are we in God's eyes? The blood Jesus shed on the cross washed our sins away and in God's eyes we are whiter than snow. Therefore, God says that He does not remember our sins. He called us righteous. Therefore, now, is our judgment of what we've seen correct, or is God's judgment correct?

Many people do not incline their ears to the Word of God, but instead follow their thoughts and call themselves sinners. They think that doing so and praying for forgiveness and doing good deeds is being truthful. It may seem so, but objectively put, such things come about from distrusting the Word of God.

## Now Let Us Become People Who Believe God

You must throw your thoughts away to live true spiritual life. When you stand with sadness or misery, think, "God, is this the case in your eyes also?" Go to God and ask, "God, is this misery? Is this sadness? Is this pain?" Then if God does say that it is sadness, it is. But even though it looks like misery in your eyes, if God calls it joy, do not believe yourself and believe that it is joy. This is believing God.

Because God's heart is different from your own, you cannot believe God if you follow your own heart. Many people go to church and are agonizing over sin. It is because they cannot believe that Jesus took care of their sin. Jesus shed His blood on the cross to free us from sin so that we may not agonize over it. The blood of Jesus lacks nothing in washing our sins away. No matter what dirty sin it is, He washed all the sin of mankind clean at the cross.

Satan deceives our hearts to make us think that Jesus could not forgive our sins. That is why there are many people who, with darkness in their hearts, live tied down to sin.

Now I hope that you will change your heart. In your eyes surely you are a sinner, but the Bible says that you are righteous. It says that He does not remember your sins anymore. It says that your sins have been blotted like the clouds that disappear and the fog that disappears. If so, your sins truly are blotted out. When you do not believe in yourself, but believe in the Word of God and live freed from sin, the Holy Spirit will work with power in you.

Loving folks, until now you have believed in yourself, but now I hope you will become people who can believe in God. Deny yourself and accept the Word of God. So regardless of what your thoughts are, say, "If God says that I am righteous, I am righteous. God has called me clean. My sins are washed as white as snow. God does not remember my sins anymore."

Throw away the many thoughts that follow along. I hope that you can establish this heart in you to be able to live the blessed life through faith.

# 48

# *The Genealogy of Esau That Changed from Life to Death*

*Now these are the generations of Esau, who is Edom. Esau took his wives of the daughters of Canaan; Adah the daughter of Elon the Hittite, and Aholibamah the daughter of Anah the daughter of Zibeon the Hivite; And Bashemath Ishmael's daughter, sister of Nebajoth. And Adah bare to Esau Eliphaz; and Bashemath bare Reuel; And Aholibamah bare Jeush, and Jaalam, and Korah: these are the sons of Esau, which were born unto him in the land of Canaan.* (Genesis 35:16~18)

## The Genealogies of the Bible

When we first start reading the Bible, in the beginning it seems difficult and frustrating. But as we continue reading, we begin to witness a current flowing throughout. For example, Moses met his wife Zipporah at a well. Jacob also first met his wife Rachel at a well. Abraham's old servant also met Abraham's daughter-in-law, Rebekah, at a well. When we read the Bible throughout and see that all the brides were found at a well, we come to realize, "Ah, the well represents the bride." We can see such currents when we read the Bible and we are able to realize and understand it.

Just as there are clear meanings in the Bible, there are certain parts that are connected with others. I read the genealogies thinking that they were simply records of genealogies. When I read the genealogy of Jesus in Matthew chapter 1, I used to think, "Is the Bible trying to teach us patience?" because all it talked about was who begat who and so forth. But as I read it many times, there were things the Holy Spirit made me realize.

*The book of the generations of Jesus Christ, the son of David, the son of Abraham. Abraham begat Isaac; and Isaac begat Jacob; and Jacob begat Judas and his brethren; and Judas begat Phares and Zara of Thamar, and Phares begat Esrom; and Esrom begat Aram. . . .*(Matthew 1:1-3)

In the genealogy of Jesus Christ are the works of life, saying, " . . . begat, begat . . . " and the word death is not once used. It wasn't just written this way, but it was written so for a reason. There is no death if one enters into the genealogy of Jesus. It is telling us that if you are in the genealogy of Jesus Christ, you will not taste death but gain everlasting life.

On the contrary, how is the genealogy of Adam recorded in the Old Testament? It says this in Genesis chapter 5.

*And Adam lived an hundred and thirty years, and begat a son in his own likeness, after his image; and called his name Seth: And the days of Adam after he had begotten Seth were eight hundred years: and he begat sons and daughters. And all the days that Adam lived were nine hundred and thirty years: and he died.* (Genesis 5:3-5)

The genealogy of Adam mentions death. There are life and death in this genealogy.

There is something very interesting in the genealogy of Esau in Genesis chapter 36 as well, of which we will be talking today. The whole of Genesis chapter 36 is the genealogy of Esau. When the genealogy of Esau begins in the first part of verse 4, it starts with the works of life, saying, *And Adah bare to Esau, Eliphaz; and Bashemath bare Reuel; And Aholibamah bare Jeush, and Jalaam, and Korah. . . .* However, as there were more and more tribes, it says from verse 15, *These were the dukes of the sons of Esau: the sons of Eliphaz, the first-born of*

*Esau; duke Teman, duke Omar, duke Zepho, duke Kenaz. . . .* Dukes were continually formed, a hierarchy was formed, and systems were formed. From then on, the word "begat" no longer appears. If we go a little further, it says, *And these are the kings that reigned in the land of Edom, before there reigned any king over the children of Israel,* in verse 31. They began simply but went on to have dukes. Then they went one step further and began to have kings. The systems are well placed, but something interesting begins in verse 32: *And Bela the son of Beor reigned in the land of Edom, before there reigned any king over the children of Israel. And Bela died, and Jobab the son of Zerah of Borzah reigned in his stead.*

The genealogy of Esau is divided into three levels. In the first level they begin in simplicity and there were the works of life. In the middle level they begin to have dukes, and it no longer speaks of life or death. Then finally, when they had kings, it no longer speaks of birth but only words of death continue. God didn't write the Bible randomly this way. When people make tombstones, they write when a person was born and when he died. God made each genealogy different when He wrote the Scriptures. In some genealogies only life reigns while in some genealogies death reigns. In some genealogies, death and life are fighting one another.

## Tommy the Drug Addict's Change

If one enters the genealogy of Jesus in Matthew chapter 1, there is no death there. This was so amazing to me. After Jesus Christ entered my life, the sting of death was sin, but Jesus pushed all my sins out. Before, I was one who begat death, begat sin, and begat darkness. But as Jesus entered me, I was only myself on the outside. I had died and I lived with the heart of Jesus which I never had before. Then things like the works of Jesus began to happen in my life.

I once preached the gospel to a man who had been addicted to drugs for more than 40 years. He told me all about how he had done drugs and said how filthy and dirty he had lived and said to me, "Pastor, your sermon tonight struck my heart." I spoke to him about the growth of a butterfly.

"Do you know how a caterpillar becomes a butterfly? It is not a beautiful caterpillar that becomes a butterfly. A disgusting, filthy caterpillar becomes a beautiful butterfly. Likewise, God is trying to make us, who are filthy and evil, into the precious sons of God."

He laughed, saying, "Me? Become a butterfly?" I spoke once again.

"Right now, in your heart, you believe this cannot be because you believe in your own heart. However, you must receive Jesus into your heart. With your heart, you cannot be free from drugs or free from sin. With your thoughts or calculations, you cannot reach Jesus' heart. We have to leave the earth to reach the moon. We can never get there if we are still sitting on earth. Likewise, because our nature is filthy and dirty, we can only live dirty and filthy lives if we remain in ourselves. You have to be freed from your thoughts if you want to change. You have to distrust and deny yourself. You have to open the Bible, and regardless of how your thoughts are, you have to listen to what the word is saying."

I opened to Jeremiah chapter 17, verse 9 and spoke to him.

*The heart is deceitful above all things and desperately wicked;*

"God does not say that your actions or habits are bad. God does not speak of your hypocritical, lustful actions, but He said that your heart is deceitful above all things and desperately wicked. Don't just listen to these words that say so but see the heart of God who has expressed that your heart is this way. God said that you are dirty and wicked. Can you produce goodness by simply trying with your dirty and wicked heart? Never! That is why you have to throw that heart away."

I opened to another part of the Bible and continued.

"All the works shown in the Bible began when man changed his heart. Abraham thought he could not have a son, but after believing in God's promise, he changed his heart, saying, 'If God works, I can have a son even though I am old,' and had a son. All the works in the Bible happened when the people did not trust in their hearts, but accepted the Word of God and changed their hearts. What does the Bible say? You are filthy and dirty, but the Bible says that you are already made righteous. Even before you knew it, He cleansed you through the blood Jesus shed on the cross. When you accept this into your heart, you are righteous. You have already been made righteous, and now it is simply letting this come upon your heart.

It takes hundreds of millions of light years for the light of the stars we see to reach us. When the light reaches our eyes, we can know of its existence. Even before the light entered into our eyesight, the star existed. Likewise, our sins were already forgiven when Jesus shed His blood on the cross. However, we remain in darkness until God's heart of forgiveness reaches us. God is trying to deliver that heart to ours through the Bible. People who have that heart delivered to them; people who have seen the light of God accept that their sins have been washed away. But people who have not accepted the word, and people to whom the light of God had not reached remain in darkness; remain in their own thoughts."

Tommy, who had been using drugs for 40 years, met Jesus that day. Tommy had strained to become freed from drugs, but had failed. However, Jesus entered him. Of course, even after this, there was the temptation of drugs. Once, his leg was hurt as he was hit by a car on his way to buy drugs. He came to know that God was stopping him. Then he got in a wheelchair to buy drugs but got into a fight with the drug dealers. They became angry and picked him up in his wheelchair and threw him into a garbage dump and he thought he was going to die. Right then he changed his heart. From that day on he changed into someone who quit drugs and preached the gospel.

He did not fight to quit drugs. When Jesus entered his heart, Jesus cast the drugs far away from him. When there were oxen, sheep, and doves in the temple of Jerusalem, no one could cast them out but Jesus. In the temple of your heart, you will fail miserably if you try to fight against the darkness, dirtiness, filthiness, and wickedness, but will win if Jesus fights them.

Moving into genealogies represents moving the heart. A woman may ponder, "Shall I live with this man, or that man?" But if she decides to marry a person named A, she will move into his genealogy. Likewise, if you live with your thoughts you remain in Adam's genealogy and must live a life where death ever continues. If a married woman becomes divorced and then marries into another family, she becomes a woman of that genealogy. Bathsheba was such a woman. Harlot Rachab was such a woman. She who had relationships with all sorts of men entered Salmon's genealogy and united her heart with him. It is not important that we go to church, but that we receive the heart of Jesus. If we throw away the heart to believe in ourselves and accept the heart of Jesus Christ, we receive truly amazing grace through Jesus.

## Systems Who Replaced God in Our Heart

*And these are the kings that reigned in the land of Edom, before there reigned any king over the children of Israel.* (Genesis 36:31)

Esau's tribe had advanced. Before Israel had a king, already the Kingdom of Edom was standing. Israel went long without a king because they had God. Even when they were establishing their first king, Saul, God wanted Himself to be king; He was not pleased with Saul becoming king. When they did not have God, they had to organize and make systems. Because Israel had God, the people lived happily through the prophets.

It seems that having a king would help a country, but rather, it caused much loss. Political systems today establish representatives because they are necessary. But if we all are ruled by God, if God becomes the king in our heart, we do not need any other king. The tribe of Esau established a king who was not God. Afterward, the works of death continued with them. It seemed on the outside that they were advancing and becoming better, but in reality, the works of death were continuing with them. That is what political advancement brings.

When the Pilgrims first set foot on America, they arrived despite many difficulties. That year, they lost all of their crops to the wind. They were attacked by Indians. They caught fevers. They prayed to God in these times of difficulties. They first built churches, prayed, and farmed despite the difficulties, and observed a day of Thanksgiving. There was God at the core of their heart. Afterwards, through the blessing of God, America became wealthier and more powerful. Through this their systems improved as well. Now they have welfare systems, retirement systems, insurance systems. . . . Everything became better.

Recently someone said to me, "God has left the American heart and is replaced with insurance companies." Before, when there was fire, diseases, or accidents, they would rely on God. But now when they call the insurance company, it takes care of everything for them. Fire insurance for fire, medical insurance for sickness, unemployment insurance for unemployment. . . . In this way, as systems improved, many lost the opportunity to seek God. It seemed in the beginning to be good because of convenience, but these things ultimately took away the path to discover God; the path to find God. Now they are so distant from God that they are unable to find God even though they have no other way. They have no choice but to flow in human methods. As this kind of life continued, America began to corrupt.

### To Have Us Not Stand on Our Own

We have to go forward toward God. There were works of

birth in the genealogy of Esau in Genesis chapter 36, but later it continued to the works of death. When I first married, we had no home; we had nothing. Our house did not have a coat hanger, and one day we bought one from the store, and it was so nice to have one. When we first bought the electric rice cooker, I remember how joyful my wife was. Back then we lived relying on God. Back then we had to pray to God to ask for travel fare if we had to go somewhere. Nowadays, our lives have gotten better and we can just take our car. Everything has become better. The thankful thing is, now there is nothing I need to pray for in terms of my life, but there are greater things instead that I have to pray about. I have to pray concerning the many great difficulties that arise while we preach the gospel in Korea and all over the world. Rather than setting up systems to take care of these problems smoothly, it is so great that I can look to and rely on God.

As we talked about last time, Rachel had nothing to seek God about because she was perfect and Leah could only seek God because she was lacking. God made us weak. God could have made us strong like the panther, or like the lion. He could have made us big like the elephant and He could have made our hearts strong also. However, why did He make us to be so weak and why did He make our hearts so weak that we fall into sin and become disappointed when tempted? It was to have us not stand on our own but stand through believing in Jesus Christ. But we continually try to establish ourselves. We try to form systems so that we can live well without Jesus and we are establishing that kind of a kingdom. It seems that our lives are becoming better, but we are becoming distant from God.

## Moving into the Genealogy of Jesus Christ

This is the lesson from the genealogy of Adam, the genealogy of Esau, and the genealogy of Jesus Christ. Do not be happy that you live abundantly in a nice home. This becomes the gateway to become distant from God. Also, do not be sad or discouraged because you do not have fuel to burn today or are hungry due to lack of food. If you can seek God through these things, then they are things that are truly precious and beautiful.

God is teaching us many things through the Bible. If we were good, with that goodness we would not have been able to receive the goodness of God. But our goodness to a certain extent looks good, but is not perfect. We have to throw all our good away for us to accept God's goodness; Jesus' goodness. This is what the Bible is precisely telling us.

There is life in the genealogy of Jesus Christ. Jesus destroyed death. When Jesus went to Jairus' house, his daughter was dead, but He cast death out. Death could no longer remain there. When the old widow's son died, Jesus cast death out and he came to life. When Jesus went to Lazarus' tomb and cast death out, death ended there.

Even though your life may be in darkness, filthiness, destitution, and even though you are walking in the valley of the shadow of death, Jesus will brighten the valley of death and have you be blessed if He is with you. The life of entering the genealogy of Jesus Christ; the life of moving your heart into Jesus; the life of trusting not yourself but trusting Jesus is the truly blessed and beautiful life.

# 49

## *The New Born Again Life*

*And Joseph dreamed a dream, and he told it his brethren: and they hated him yet the more. And he said unto them, Hear, I pray you, this dream which I have dreamed: For, behold, we were binding sheaves in the field, and, lo, my sheaf arose, and also stood upright; and, behold, your sheaves stood round about, and made obeisance to my sheaf. And his brethren said to him, Shalt thou indeed reign over us? or shalt thou indeed have dominion over us? And they hated him yet the more for his dreams, and for his words. And he dreamed yet another dream, and told it his brethren, and said, Behold, I have dreamed a dream more; and, behold, the sun and the moon and the eleven stars made obeisance to me.* (Genesis 37:5-9)

## The Accurate Diagnosis

People who do not know spiritual life for the most part think that if they pray diligently, read the Bible, keep the law, and be good their spiritual life will go well. But one needs to receive an accurate diagnosis of his spiritual life if he is to live true spiritual life.

I was once hospitalized. There were red spots appearing on my buttocks which then spread through my entire body. Someone visiting me saw these and said that they were from my body overheating. He told me that fresh-squeezed bean sprout juice was the best for getting rid of this kind of heat. The juice smelled terrible but I drank a lot of it anyways, but I was not healed. Another person told me that I should drink a three-bean tea made from red beans, green beans, and black beans. I did, but I was not healed at all.

So I asked to see the chief dermatologist at the hospital. The dermatologist saw me and at once said, "Ah, look at him! This is a side effect from antibiotics." He told the intern next to him, "Check his records and tell me all the antibiotics he has taken." He told me that I have to take antibiotics for antibiotic side effects, and prescribed me the medication. After having one bag of this medication, the red spots turned black and weakened. Then I was completely healed after two days. I suffered for over 15 days but I became quickly healed. It is very important to have an illness accurately diagnosed and to take the right medication.

When our spiritual life does not go well, it is very ignorant to say, "It will go well if I try harder. It will go well if I pray. It will go well if I read the Bible." We must know the exact reason spiritual life is not working.

## People Who Belong to the Flesh and People Who Belong to God

Joseph one day dreamt that the sheaves he gathered stood up while the sheaves the brothers gathered bowed down. The brothers heard of this dream and hated Joseph so much that they wanted to kill him. I cannot understand that they hated him enough to want to kill him for having this kind of a dream. This is not an ordinary story. Why did they have the heart to kill their younger brother? This is showing a spiritual world to us. We can see that the spirit of Joseph and the older brothers were different and that their hearts were flowing differently.

All people are descendants of Adam. When Adam ate the fruit of the knowledge of good and evil, he had to decide, "Will I follow the Word of God or follow the voice of Satan?" But when Jesus was tempted by the devil, He did not exert his own will but said, "For it is written . . . ," and spoke the words of God exactly as they were. Because Jesus believed the words of God and kept them in His heart verbatim, He fought through the words. However, Adam heard the Word of God, heard the words of the serpent, and decided through his own thoughts. Adam ultimately chose the words of the serpent. In other words, he threw God away. From then on Adam's heart became separated from God and connected with Satan. This is exactly the same with us, the descendants of Adam. Jesus said in John chapter 8, "Ye are of your father the devil and the lusts of your father ye will do."

You probably have tried to do good. You may have tried to be honest. You may have tried to overcome ambitions. But it has not worked. Why not? Though they live in the same green pastures, lions do not eat the grass but eat impalas or zebras. But zebras will only eat grass even if there is meat available everywhere. Just as carnivores and herbivores are completely different, there are people who belong to God and there are people who belong to the world. Even if one goes to church, is baptized, is a deacon, is an elder, or is a pastor, unless he is born again, he belongs to the world. That person's heart is led by the spirit of the world. On the contrary, people of God have God in them for the spirit of God to lead them.

People do not know this and think, "All I need to do is keep the law well, pray, and read the Bible." But people who belong to the flesh cannot live spiritual life well no matter how hard they try. That is like a lion, a panther, or a hyena trying to eat grass. These animals do not care for grass no matter how good it is but only want to capture zebras or impalas to eat them. A person who belongs to the flesh will not become a person of the spirit just by attending church. One does not become born again just because he prays. Unless one is born again through the Holy Spirit of God, a person who belongs to the flesh is still only a person of the flesh. Therefore even if he repents, prays, reads the Bible, and has the will to be good, he may do such things for a brief while as he has those thoughts. But when he forgets the dirty, lustful, and deceitful thoughts from the core of his heart spring forth, because these are the things the flesh likes. So it is with the world. One becomes bored and frustrated while reading the Bible while enjoying the stories of the world. Thus the ambitions and the pleasures of the flesh can only rule them. Such people trying to pray well, witness, and keep the law, no matter how hard they try, will not work.

## People Belonging to the Flesh Will Not Accept the Things of God

Joseph and his brothers are of the same father, but the brothers belonged to the world. They were fallen into the ambitions of the flesh of eating, drinking, and enjoying. Joseph had a different view because he was born again. The thoughts of his heart were different from others. It was because he received the heart from God. "My sheaf stood while my brothers' sheaves are bowing down. I will become governor. It would be good if my brothers would listen to me. . . . I wish my brothers would understand this and follow me. . . ."

Joseph told his brothers about his dream. Joseph wished that his brothers would hear his words and say, "Ah, he will indeed become governor and rule over us. Then we should follow him," and become born again. But the brothers rather hated him when he spoke to them about the dream. It was because they had a different spirit.

Just because the parents are born again does not mean the children are born again also. Our parents bore our flesh, but the father of our spirit is God. All must become born again through God. People become completely new when they are born again. The Bible says, "On that day the lions will eat grass like the cow," and in this manner new hearts enter our heart. Joseph lived with his brothers but one day became born again. Until then he was led by his ambition, the thoughts of Satan. But when he received the revelation from God and supplied by the spirit, he became a person who lived in a world completely different form his brothers.

This was also true with Noah. Noah lived in a lustful, riotous world but one day became a new person as he was born again through the grace of God. Now Noah was listening to the voice of God. "I will destroy the world with water." Grass is not enjoyable to lions but is enjoyable to cows. In this way, these words of God came strongly upon Noah and he accepted them into his heart. Other people also heard that God will destroy the world with water but they did not accept these words. "What flood? It will just rain a bit and stop." So when they saw Noah building the ark, they thought, "What is going on here? Why does he believe so blindly? God loves us. Why would He send rain to destroy us?"

Why didn't they build the ark? Why didn't they enter the ark? It was because they did not accept the Word of God. It means that they accepted the ambitions and pleasures from Satan. The people who belong to Satan are this way. Paul said that people who are not of the Holy Spirit and belong to the flesh do not accept the things of the flesh.

*But the natural man received not the things of the Spirit of God: for they are foolishness unto him: neither can he know them, because they are spiritually discerned.* (1 Corinthians 2:14)

Noah felt so sorry for them.

"Everyone, haven't you heard that God will destroy this earth with the flood? But why aren't you building the ark? What are you going to do when God destroys this world with a flood? You will soon be destroyed; what good is building a house and what good is building a ranch? Isn't it important to build the ark?"

"It is important. We know it's important. That is why you are building the ark. But we are okay."

There is one thing that is a little disappointing about the Bible. I would like to put this into the Bible: when the ark was complete and God was sending the rain, the screams of the people, "Ah! Noah was right! We despised the Word of God! That is why we are destroyed!" Such screams, there must have been screams of, "Why didn't I listen to the Word of God!" when they were running away alone as they saw their wives and children being wiped away by the water. I want to put such screams into the Bible. The scary thing is that Satan has hid such things. That is why even though death comes upon man, people do not accept the Word of God.

## Then the Uprooting Repentance Occurs

Ever since I was young I learned about repentance at church. At that time the repentance I learned was, "God, I lied. I stole. I hated others," and begging for forgiveness. I thought that was repentance. But later on as I read the Bible I came to know that that was not true repentance. Theft, murder, and adultery are results of the heart of the flesh. You have to have lust in your heart for it to develop into adultery. Covetousness develops into theft, and hatred develops into murder. Try to stab your own eye with a knife. How could you stab your own loving eye? If you love you can never kill.

True repentance the Bible talks about is not committing adultery, murder, and theft and then confessing of them. No matter how much you try to not steal, commit adultery, or murder, how can you not do them when those hearts arise in you? When the heart to lust does not arise in you when you see a woman, you cannot commit adultery even if you want to. If you have no covetousness how could you steal, and without hatred how could you kill? This is the relationship of the tree and the fruit. The tree of sin bears the fruits of sin, but the problem lies in the type of repentance where the fruits of sin are merely plucked off. No matter how much you pluck, there is no end. Therefore people always sin and repent, and live sinning and repenting. You pluck one fruit, another is borne, pluck another fruit, and another is borne. The tree must be uprooted with an ax but people try to do good while keeping the evilness at the core of their hearts.

I attended church but for a very long time that was how I

lived my spiritual life. "I should be good, I should not lie, I should not have a lustful heart, I should not steal. . . ." But it did not work. My actions were somewhat controlled, but I could not do anything about the dirty desires and ambitions of my heart. But I thought I was good. But one day God gave me His grace and allowed me to precisely see my image of having fallen inside sin. At that moment, I think God allowed me to borrow His eyes. Until then I saw myself and thought I was truthful and smart. But my image seen in the eyes of God was a dirty, filthy human being worthy to be cursed and destroyed. Right then I knew. "This is how the core of my heart is. What good could I do? Even if I were to do good, it would be fake. This is how evil and dirty my heart is. How could I serve God?" I discovered that I was a filthy human who could only be destroyed.

Right then all of the heart to believe in myself crumbled down. After knowing how truly evil my thoughts were, I came to distrust myself. Before, I always believed my thoughts and followed my thoughts more than the Word of God. But as I denied myself, the precious grace appeared. I believed that my sins were forgiven through the blood of Jesus. Before, I said that the blood of Jesus forgave my sins but it seemed my sins remained. But as I precisely believed that Jesus forgave all of my sins, my heart began to change. Jesus had come inside me.

What a wonderful change in my life has been wrought, since Jesus came into my heart.

From then on I who enjoyed the ambitions of the world liked the Bible so much and it was so graceful that I read it every day. Sometimes I needed to run some errands but had a little time left. I would think to read the Bible for a moment but I would forget everything and read the Bible all day long until the sunset. The Bible was so graceful. When a lion becomes a cow, the grass becomes delicious. Likewise, I changed and the Word of God began to live and work inside me. I was completely changed.

## New Born Again Man, Joseph

Joseph was a changed person. The Bible does not tell us the details of how he changed, but the brothers heard the voice of the world, the voice of the devil while Joseph heard the voice of God and received the guidance of God. Therefore what Joseph saw was completely different from what the brothers saw.

Joseph dreamt again. He saw that the eleven stars of the heavens, and the sun and the moon were bowing to him.

"Okay, let me tell my brothers about this dream. Then my brothers will change their hearts and may believe God."

"Hello, brothers."

"You punk, are you gonna tell us about dreams again?"

"Yes, I had another dream."

"Did you have a different dream this time? Did you dream that you became a slave?"

"No, I dreamt that eleven stars, the sun, and the moon bowed down to me."

"What did you say? I thought you changed your heart . . . You punk!"

Joseph thought upon hearing this, the brothers would say, "Ah, you will indeed become the governor. When it happens, have mercy on us. Then what should we do now?" But the brothers hated Joseph so much they wanted to kill him.

This was how Apostle Paul was before he was born again. He hated born again people so much that he killed them. Satan deceived him to make him this way.

Joseph's brothers set up a plan to kill Joseph. But after Joseph became governor, he did not hate his brothers. The brothers felt that surely Joseph will hate them for trying to kill him and thought he would set out to kill them. But Joseph's heart was different. Joseph had received the heart of God, and the heart of Jesus. The love inside Jesus overcomes hatred and thus Joseph could not hate. The righteousness inside the heart of Jesus defeats sin and thus sin cannot remain. Holiness defeats filthiness. This does not come about through effort but this accomplishes the holy life.

Joseph is showing us the image of a born again, new person. Everything he did was prosperous and blessed. Joseph had the broad heart of Jesus to forgive his brothers who tried to kill him. On the contrary, the brothers had the evil heart to kill Joseph, which shows us that the evil spirit and the Holy Spirit of God are different.

## Ye Must Be Born Again

People think, "I have to pray hard. I have to read the Bible," but Jesus said that man cannot see the kingdom of God unless he is born again. Being born again is being cut off from the wild olive tree and being grafted on to the true olive tree. Just as David said, "I was shapen in iniquity and in sin did my mother conceive me," because your heart is evil and only filthy, you must distrust your heart and accept the heart of Jesus. Then you can live blessedly through the heart of Jesus.

Loving folks, you should not simply try hard but become born again. We by nature are filthy and dirty from the seed of Adam. We should distrust our thoughts and accept the heart of Jesus, so that as the day for lions to eat grass comes, we can live the bright, joyful, new life through God.